REST-EASY RETIREMENT

REST-EASY RETIREMENT

THE TRUTH
ABOUT ANNUITIES

SCOTT STOLZ

Advantage | Books

Published by Advantage, Charleston, South Carolina.
Member of Advantage Media.

ADVANTAGE is a registered trademark, and the Advantage colophon is a trademark of Advantage Media Group, Inc.

Printed in the United States of America.

10 9 8 7 6 5 4 3 2 1

ISBN: 978-1-64225-763-2 (Paperback)
ISBN: 978-1-64225-423-5 (eBook)

LCCN: 2023902166

Cover design by Matthew Morse.
Layout design by Matthew Morse.

This publication is designed to provide accurate and authoritative information in regard to the subject matter covered. It is sold with the understanding that the publisher is not engaged in rendering legal, accounting, or other professional services. If legal advice or other expert assistance is required, the services of a competent professional person should be sought.

Advantage Media helps busy entrepreneurs, CEOs, and leaders write and publish a book to grow their business and become the authority in their field. Advantage authors comprise an exclusive community of industry professionals, idea-makers, and thought leaders. Do you have a book idea or manuscript for consideration? We would love to hear from you at **AdvantageMedia.com**.

CONTENTS

INTRODUCTION

A few years ago, I wrote *Unlocking the Annuity Mystery: Practical Advice for Every Advisor*. While I wrote this book mostly for financial advisors, I tried to make it simple enough that anyone could get at least a basic understanding of how annuities work and when and why they should be used. As a test, I asked my wife to read the book. Now, she's pretty damn smart. She owns her own business, consults to small business CEOs, and has a pretty good financial acumen. When she didn't even make it past the second chapter, I knew I had failed in writing a book that could reach beyond financial advisors. Hence, this second book. Hopefully, you (and my wife) will find this book both informative and easy to read.

Eventually you will "retire." Or maybe you are already "retired." I put "retired" within quotation marks because retirement means different things to different people. For some, it means not working at all. For others, it means just working less or only doing what you really want to do. For me, it means not setting an alarm clock in the morning unless I want to. Regardless of your definition of retirement, it likely means you no longer have a reliable income and/or significantly less income. If you are like most people—including me—you wonder whether you will have enough money in retirement to do all the things you want to do, even if you have unexpected expenses. If you're reading this book, you have probably done some research on this subject. During this research you've probably read that many financial academics believe that, for most people, annuities should be part of the solution. Yet when you did a Google search on annuities, you probably also found posts that were highly critical of annuities right alongside those that were supportive. Further complicating the topic is that there are a lot of different annuities, most of which are designed to address different financial goals. If you found this book in hopes of getting to the bottom of all this, you have come to the right place.

I fell into the annuity industry in 1983, when, as a twenty-three-year-old newly minted MBA from Washington University in St. Louis, I was offered the position of annuity product manager by Edward Jones in St. Louis. I liked the idea of being a product manager. I only had one question: What was an annuity? Despite earning both undergraduate and graduate degrees in finance, I had been taught nothing about annuities. After accepting the job, I went looking for a book like this. I couldn't find one. In fact, despite some of the books written about annuities over the years, I still don't believe the book I was looking for back in 1983 exists today. And that is another reason why I wrote this book.

I never thought I would stay in the annuity industry more than a year or two. I assumed way back when that this first job out of college was just a stepping stone to some other role in the finance world. But one job led to another, which led to another, and so on. And so almost forty years later, I remain in the annuity industry. It would be safe to say that I've seen a lot over the years—both good and bad.

At this point it's important for you to understand that I'm pro annuities. It would be impossible to spend almost forty years in an industry if I felt otherwise. In fact, I own two myself. However, I don't believe that an annuity is for everyone. Far from it. While the annuities I own are an integral part of my retirement plan, I recognize that I had other viable options to meet my financial objectives. In any financial planning process, there is always more than one viable approach. In addition, not every annuity is created equal. Like any other investment category, some annuities are better than others. In fact, while today's annuities are more consumer-friendly than ever, there are still some individual annuities out there that are designed in such a way that the primary goal is to incentivize someone to sell them rather than to help the policyowner meet an investment and/ or retirement goal.

So why do I own two annuities? What role do they play in my investment portfolio? First and foremost, like most people, I like the idea of getting a social security check for as long as I live. Say what you want about social security, but there is a reason so many people like it. It provides peace of mind. No matter what the market does from year to year, you know that check is going to be deposited into your account every year. However, if I want to truly enjoy retirement, I'm going to need far more than what social security is going to pay me. I can find plenty of research that says I can safely supplement my retirement income by simply taking 3–4 percent of my portfolio each year. If I have $1 million, I can take $30,000–$40,000 each year with a very low probability of running out of money before I die. In fact, if I limit the withdrawals to that rate, I'll likely see my portfolio grow. But note a few key words in those two sentences: "very low probability" and "likely." I understand the math, and I know I probably (there's that word again) don't need an annuity. But I just don't want to worry about it in retirement. I want to know how much income I'm going to have, no matter what the market does and no matter how long I live. If you feel the same way, then keep reading.

But since I have not yet retired, I haven't started taking income from my annuities yet. So what have they done for me up to now? The government wants you to save for your own retirement, so it provides incentives for you to do so. For example, you get a tax deduction for any money you put into a regular IRA. In addition, you don't pay taxes while your IRA grows. No taxes are due until you take money out. In industry jargon, that is called tax deferral, since you defer the taxes until later. An annuity is similar. While I didn't get a tax deduction for the money I put into my two annuities, I haven't paid any taxes over the years on their growth. Just as importantly, I was able to move money back and forth between the various investment options in the annuities without paying any taxes. When I wanted to get more heavily invested, I sold the more conservative investment options and bought more aggressive ones. I did the opposite when I wanted to get more conservative. All without taxes. So, if you like the idea of paying less taxes while you save for retirement, keep reading.

In the end, annuities are about protection—protection of income, protection from taxes, and protection from drastic market swings. If any of these appeal to you, keep reading. I'll explain to you how this protection works and what it will cost you.

My primary goal with this book is to not to convince you that you need an annuity, but rather to give you the information you need to feel comfortable with the decisions you make. And quite frankly, if your goal is to find information that supports a critical view of annuities, you will find plenty of that in this book as well. In these pages, I will share both the good and the bad.

Spoiler alert—this is not a whodunit, so this book will be heavy on information and light (pretty much void, actually) on suspense. There's only so much I can do to make learning about annuities fun. I'll leave the fun to the Stephen Kings and the Harlan Cobens of the world.

WHY SHOULD I EVEN CONSIDER AN ANNUITY?

No one in their right mind would ever ask me to build a house for them, but if there is one thing that I know for sure, it's that I would need a lot of tools to accomplish the task. If, however, you need someone to hang a picture for you, I'm your guy. I've collected a lot of original sports art over the years, which means I'm constantly replacing one picture for another. But even a task as simple as that requires a hook, a nail, a level, a yardstick and/or tape measure, and a pencil. And always measure everything at least twice. I definitely learned that one the hard way. An annuity is just one of many tools you can use to build a retirement income portfolio. And just like there are many different hooks you can use when hanging a picture (although I can use when hanging a picture (although I

AN ANNUITY IS JUST ONE OF MANY TOOLS YOU CAN USE TO BUILD A RETIREMENT INCOME PORTFOLIO.

strongly recommend you spend the extra money for the professional picture hangers), an annuity is just one of many options that can be selected to accomplish certain goals. When it comes to investing, there is never any one best single solution. Every solution comes with trade-offs. Annuities are no different.

Annuities can help with three basic financial goals. First, they can help preserve wealth by providing protection against the ups and downs of the stock market. Second, because they compound earnings without taxation, they can help you accumulate wealth much faster than investments that are taxed each year. And finally, they can give you the peace of mind of providing a retirement income that will continue until the day you die.

Your first thought might be that I'm overselling the benefits. After all, those three things cover a lot of financial needs. However, while different annuities can meet these three major goals, annuities typically fall short of expectations when a single annuity is selected to try to accomplish two, or even all three, of these things. When I hang a picture, I just use the hammer to pound in the nail. I can also try to use it to measure the proper distance, estimate how level the hangers are, and even mark the wall where I want to put the nail, but I pretty much guarantee that such a strategy will lead to a crooked and/or misplaced picture.

Using Annuities to Preserve Wealth

Many annuities are designed specifically to protect the assets you have already accumulated from the ups and downs of the stock and bond markets. I'll go into each of the following in more detail in specific chapters on each type of annuity, but the following list highlights the basic principles.

1. *Fixed and indexed annuities will credit only a positive rate of return and will never drop in value from year to year.* Basically, both of these products serve as substitutes

to bank certificates of deposit (CDs). A fixed annuity will credit a specific, known rate of interest each year. The rate you earn will change at the end of the term which you select. An indexed annuity will credit a rate tied to a specific index, such as the S&P 500. At the end of the term you select, the insurance company will look back to see how much that index increased over that period. You will either earn the full change up to a stated limit (known as a "cap") or a specific percentage of the change (e.g., 35 percent). In exchange for giving up the certainty of knowing what rate of interest you will earn like you get with a fixed annuity, over time, an indexed annuity should earn 1–1.5 percent more per year on average compared to a fixed annuity. The most important thing with both of these types of annuities is that you will have the peace of mind of knowing that you won't have less money tomorrow than you had today.

2. **Structured annuities eliminate some of the downside risk with investing in stocks or mutual funds.** Structured annuities are the next level up in terms of risk versus reward versus fixed and indexed annuities. Rather than protect all the downsides of the market, they protect a portion of it. For example, one structured annuity in the market absorbs 50 percent of any downside movement in the stock index but gives you 70–80 percent of the upside movement. Others might limit your downside to no more than 10 percent during a specific 1–6-year period. And finally, some designs absorb the first 10–30 percent of the index losses, leaving your assets at risk only for losses greater than the designated percentage. Don't worry if you find this concept a little confusing. I'll cover these options in detail in the chapter on

structured annuities. For now just understand that if your selected stock index falls in price, the insurance company will absorb a portion of the loss.

3. *Variable annuities provide a guarantee of your initial invested amount at death.* If you are thinking, "Wow, dying is a tough price to pay for a guarantee," I wouldn't argue the point. However, if you stop and think about it, there's actually a great deal of logic for this strategy. It's not uncommon for people to have money that they don't expect to need during retirement and that they plan to leave to others. Naturally, they want that money to grow, but at the same time they want to preserve a minimum value for whomever is to get it when they die. If the money is put in stocks or mutual funds, over time it will most certainly grow. But there is also a possibility that those stocks or mutual funds could be down in value when you die—especially if you die not long after you bought them. If instead you invest in mutual funds via a variable annuity, you know that the minimum your heirs will get is whatever you put into the annuity, adjusted for withdrawals, if any, of course.

Using Annuities to Control Taxes

Before I cover the tax advantages of annuities, I have to introduce two more financial terms: "qualified" money and "nonqualified" money. Money is considered "qualified" if it resides in a retirement plan such as an IRA, Roth IRA, 403(b), or 401(k). These plans all "qualify" for special tax treatment under the tax code, hence the industry referring to them as qualified assets. Similarly, an IRA is considered a qualified plan. Any asset held in a retirement account, including annuities, gets taxed under the tax rules of that particular retirement plan. The tax aspects of the plan override any special tax considerations of any assets in the plan. Therefore, there is no tax advantage to one product over another when it is held within that plan. Every asset in an IRA, for example, is taxed completely the same. Any asset that is not held in a qualified plan is considered a nonqualified asset. Any account you might have with a brokerage firm or bank that is not part of a retirement account would therefore be considered a nonqualified account. Even your checking account would be an example of a nonqualified asset, as would an account where you just own stocks, bonds, or mutual funds. If an asset is a nonqualified asset, it is taxed according to the terms of that asset as well as potentially the amount of time you owned the asset.

Annuities are given their own special tax treatment under the tax code. In order to encourage people to save for retirement and put money into something that can provide an income for life, the tax code allows all nonqualified annuities to be tax deferred. Common sense tells us that it's better to pay taxes later than now. Think of it this way: Let's assume it's April 15, and your tax return tells you that you still owe $10,000 more in taxes. But just as you are starting to get out your checkbook to write that check, you get a call from the president of the United States. He or she tells you that since you have been such an outstanding citizen during the past year, you don't have to pay those taxes right now. You can pay them whenever you want. And you won't owe any more. You will still owe just $10,000. Would you write that check? Unless you just don't want to have to worry about it down the road, you wouldn't. At the very least, you could put that $10,000 into an account paying interest (such as a fixed or indexed annuity—or CD) and then earn money on the money you would have paid in taxes. That's what tax deferral does for you. It allows you to not only earn money on your original investment plus any interest you've earned to date but also earn money on the money you would have paid in taxes each year. Only tax deferral gives you the full impact of compounding interest.

Variable annuities also carry an extra tax advantage. Most of today's variable annuities offer up to one hundred or more different mutual fund type accounts. If you sell a regular mutual fund in order to buy another—perhaps because you want to increase or decrease the overall risk in your portfolio—you create a taxable gain (or loss) at the time of the sale. However, if you make that same switch by selling one of the mutual fund options within the variable annuity in order to buy another mutual fund option within that same product, no taxes are due because you can do all this within the annuity. This makes a variable annuity a very useful and tax-efficient vehicle for someone who frequently rebalances their portfolio holdings—which should be almost everyone.

One very important consideration is the fact that any taxable withdrawals from an annuity prior to age fifty-nine-and-a-half are not only taxed, but they also carry an additional 10 percent penalty. In reality this penalty is an additional 10 percent tax. Therefore, if you are in a 20 percent tax bracket, taxable annuity withdrawals will be taxed at 30 percent. As stated earlier, the government allows annuities to be tax deferred in order to encourage you to save for retirement. Therefore, the 10 percent penalty serves as a deterrent to taking money out before retirement.

Using Annuities to Give You a Paycheck for Life

Everyone loves a pension. What's not to like? There's something very reassuring about knowing that a specific sum of money is going to be deposited into your checking account each month. That also explains why social security is so sacred. Most people don't think of social security as a pension, but at the end of the day, that's exactly what it is. You have money taken out of each paycheck during your working life. In exchange, beginning sometime between the ages of sixty-two and seventy (your choice), the government promises to start sending you a check each month for as long as you live.

When an annuity is used for income, it is essentially a personal pension that you fund out of your retirement savings. You give the insurance company a sum of money—either in a lump sum or payments over a number of years—and in exchange it gives you an income for life. It's really as simple as that. In addition, if the annuity is funded with money that is not in a retirement plan—those nonqualified dollars—then the income is partly tax free. I'll go into this in more detail on the chapter on annuity taxation, but the concept is similar to any mortgage payments you make. Each mortgage payment is partly a return of the amount you borrowed and partly a return of interest. Nonqualified annuities work the same way. Each payment you receive is partly a return of the money you gave to the insurance company and partly interest that the insurance company is paying to you. You only pay taxes on the interest portion. Therefore, if you receive $20,000 in total annuity payments

> **WHEN AN ANNUITY IS USED FOR INCOME, IT IS ESSENTIALLY A PERSONAL PENSION THAT YOU FUND OUT OF YOUR RETIREMENT SAVINGS.**

in a particular year, it's likely that only half or less of those payments are taxable. The exact amount depends on when you start receiving the income, your life expectancy, and the amount of interest the insurance company expects to pay you during your lifetime.

Final Thoughts

Throughout this book, I'll cover all the things annuities can do for you in much more detail than presented in this chapter. And of course, I'll also tell you what they don't do particularly well. However, the three solutions listed in this chapter are the primary benefits offered by annuities. If none of these three interest you, you can stop reading right now. If, on the other hand, you see how one or more of the three can help you reach your financial goals, keep reading. You'll be glad you did.

WHY DO SO MANY PEOPLE HATE ANNUITIES?

If you google "are annuities a good investment," one or more of the top responses is going to be highly critical of annuities. In fact, Fisher Investments, one of the country's largest investment advisory firms, has created an entire campaign around the supposed stupidity of buying annuities. On the other end of the spectrum, some financial advisors believe that an annuity and the guaranteed income it can provide should have a place in almost everyone's retirement income plan. Like almost all controversial topics, the truth lies somewhere in the middle of these two extremes. No one can really deny that annuities have a history of being both mis-sold and oversold. In addition, the insurance companies have learned over the years that the higher the commission they pay to an advisor to sell an annuity, the more sales they get. Therefore, they have occasionally designed products that benefit those recommending the annuity as much, if not more, than those buying the annuity. Of course, this is not a concept that is unique to annuities. Commissions exist to both reward and motivate the person who is selling the product. This natural conflict of interest is bound to lead to some unsuitable sales no matter what product is being sold. With that in mind, no book on annuities would be complete without exploring the issues that have caused Fisher Investments and others to so publicly and vehemently come out against annuities.

Annuities Are Too Costly

When critics claim that annuities are too costly, they are typically referring to *variable annuities*. While almost all annuities—and certainly all commissionable annuities—assess a "surrender charge" if you get out early (more on that in a minute), variable annuities assess annual policy fees in addition to a possible surrender charge. They will assess an annual contract cost of 1–1.5 percent per year, plus a management fee on the variable annuity subaccounts of 0.5–1.25 percent per year, plus 0.5–1.5 percent for any additional income or death benefits. Consequently, a variable annuity with features added on could cost 3–3.5 percent per year. In a world where you can now buy stock for no commission and buy an index fund for

AN INSURANCE COMPANY INCURS THREE COSTS WHEN ISSUING AN ANNUITY, ALL OF WHICH ARE GOING TO BE PASSED ONTO THE ANNUITY BUYER IN ONE FORM OR ANOTHER.

almost no annual management cost, that's a large annual expense. Therefore, it is always important that you know what you are paying for each and every feature of the annuity—particularly variable annuities.

What goes into the cost of an annuity, and how do you know whether you are paying too much? An insurance company incurs three costs when issuing an annuity, all of which are going to be passed onto the annuity buyer in one form or another. The higher those costs for the insurance company, the more you will pay:

1. **Commission:** Over 95 percent of all the annuities sold pay a commission of 3–10 percent to the agent or advisor that is selling the annuity. While this is a wide range, the typical commission is closer to 3 percent than 10 percent. This commission is not deducted from your investment directly. If you buy a $100,000 annuity, your entire $100,000 will be invested on your behalf. The insurance company pays the commission out of its own pocket and then recovers it over time from either the annual charge on the contract or the difference on what they earn compared to what they pay you. For example, most variable annuities carry an annual charge of about 1.25 percent on your total investment each year. About half of that annual charge exists as a way to recover the commission the insurance company paid. On most other forms of annuities, there is no explicit charge on your account. Instead, the insurance company simply pays you less than what they can earn on the money you give them. This is known as the "spread." The larger the commission that is paid, the higher the spread. Therefore, rather than paying for the commission via a direct fee, you pay for it by earning less interest than you otherwise would have. Obviously, the higher the commission that is paid, the more future earnings you will give up. Annuities are far from the only financial vehicle that uses the concept of a spread. For example, when you buy a CD from your local bank, the bank will earn more on your deposit than what they pay you. The difference is the bank's spread. It covers not only the profits the bank earns on

your money but the costs to issue the certificate—including paying those that helped you with the purchase.

2. **Marketing and sales:** Annuities are sold, not bought. It's rare for anyone to go directly to an insurance company's website to buy an annuity. Therefore, the insurance company must do sales campaigns, print brochures, and hire staff to train the financial advisors on the products, and maybe even help them sell it. This infrastructure can get expensive. This is another cost that you will pay either directly or indirectly.

3. **Administrative:** There is a lot involved in issuing and providing ongoing service on annuity. The insurance company has to process your application and issue an actual policy. Sadly, both of these processes typically still involve paper. And then they have to send you statements, cut you checks, make occasional policy changes, have a staff available to handle your phone calls, etc.

Of these expenses, the commission is the biggest. You probably noticed that I gave a pretty big commission range. While commissions on annuities, like most other investment vehicles, have come down over time, there are still some contracts out there that can pay up to 10 percent. Typically though, reasonable commission ranges would be as follows:

- Fixed annuities: 1.5–4 percent
- Immediate annuities: 4 percent
- Indexed annuities: 3.5–5 percent
- Structured annuities: 5–6 percent
- Variable annuities: 5–7 percent

It's Costly to Get Out of an Annuity Early

All commissionable annuities are going to have a penalty for early withdrawal, commonly referred to as a "surrender charge." This is not unlike a penalty for early withdrawal that banks assess on CDs. Remember, the insurance company invests every dollar you give them and pays the commission out of its own pocket. They recover this commission over time with either the policy fees or by factoring the cost of this commission in the spread. However, depending upon the annuity design, this recovery can take five to ten years. Therefore, the insurance company assesses a charge if you get out of the contract in the first five to ten years. For this reason, this surrender charge is also sometimes referred to as a "contingent deferred sales charge." This surrender charge typically starts at 6–8 percent, and then will decline by about 1 percent per year until it completely goes away. Since the primary purpose of the surrender charge is to recover the commission paid, the amount of the initial surrender charge is also a good indicator of the commission that is paid on the contract. Simply subtract 1–2 percent from the size of the initial surrender charge, and you will be really close to the total commission.

An increasing number of annuities is being made available for fee-based accounts and therefore pay no commission to the advisor or agent. Instead, the advisor will assess an annual advisory fee just as they would for any asset within the advisory account. The amount of this fee will vary by advisor, but 0.75–1.25 percent per year would be the most common structure. Annuities sold without a commission are referred to as advisory annuities. Because these pay no commissions, they do not have a surrender charge. There is one notable exception. Most advisory indexed annuities will carry a slight surrender charge for the first few years. A typical charge might start at 4 percent and drop 1 percent per year. The purpose of this charge is not to recover the cost of the commission, but rather to allow the insurance company to buy the securities it has to buy in order to make sure they can pay you interest in the years where the market goes up, without reducing the value of your investment in the years the market goes down. If you get out of the contract early, the insurance company has to liquidate these securities in order to give you your money back. They have no guarantee that they will be able to sell these securities for at least what they paid for them; therefore, this nominal charge is designed to protect the insurance company from the possibility that they will be forced to sell these securities at a loss due to your decision to get out of the contract early.

Annuities Are Illiquid

This critique is really a subset of the section above. Regulators commonly refer to annuities as *illiquid* investments—meaning they can't be readily turned into cash. In actuality, this is not true. You can cash in your annuity any time you want. All you have to do is ask the insurance company to send you your money. You will likely need to fill out a form, but that's pretty much it. What the regulators really mean when they call an annuity illiquid is that you might have to pay a surrender charge to get out (see above), and you will likely have to pay taxes on the money you receive. Both of these can indeed be true. If you are still within the surrender charge period when you request your money, you will pay a fee to get your money. In addition, if you cash the check the insurance company sends you, you will have to pay income taxes on any amounts received above and beyond what you invested. And, if you are younger than fifty-nine-and-a-half years old, you will pay an additional 10 percent tax penalty on that income.

But these two situations are not always true. First, once you have owned the annuity long enough that you are past the surrender-charge period, you can get any amount you want with no fee at all. And even prior to that date, almost every annuity allows you to take 10 percent of your account value each year with no fee. Second, what if you own the annuity within your IRA? In fact, about half of all annuities sit in an IRA account. If this is the case, then as long as you keep the proceeds within the IRA, there are no taxes due. The taxes would be due only if

> **FROM A TAX STANDPOINT, ANNUITIES IN AN IRA ARE NO MORE ILLIQUID THAN ANY OTHER INVESTMENT IN THAT IRA.**

you withdrew the funds not only from the annuity, but the IRA as well. But that is the case with any investment in your IRA. From a tax standpoint, annuities in an IRA are no more illiquid than any other investment in that IRA.

What the regulators mean when they say that an annuity is illiquid is that it should not be the first asset you tap into in the event you have an unexpected need for cash. And that is absolutely true. Common sense would say that the best source for an unexpected need for cash is the asset you could liquidate at the lowest cost and with the least amount of taxes. Annuities would never be toward the top of this list. This is also why you should not buy an annuity outside of your IRA account unless you are confident you won't need to touch those funds until the latter of these two options: in ten years' time or when you turn fifty-nine-and-a-half.

Annuities Are Complex

It's hard to argue with this point. While the general concept of an annuity is pretty simple, with every feature that can be added to an annuity, complexity grows. Take a fixed annuity that might pay 4.5 percent per year for just three years. That in itself is far from complex. But even this simple annuity design is likely going to have both a surrender charge and market value adjustment should you get out early. And if that fixed annuity allows you to add an income benefit, the degree of complexity is increased exponentially. In addition, that annuity is going to come with a twenty-plus–page contract with lots of legal language. Any variable or structured annuity is also going to come with a prospectus that is going to be fifty-plus pages long. I've seen variable annuity prospectuses that measure more than two hundred pages.

I'd be willing to bet that fewer than 10 percent of annuity policyholders could confidently describe how their annuity works. However, the implication of this criticism is that complexity is automatically bad. Certainly, there are benefits to simplicity. But much of the complexity that comes with annuities is due to the many features and options that are available. The first cell phones were pretty simple because the only function they served was to place and receive calls. By comparison, today's cell phones are much more complex. While they can still be used to place and receive calls, for most users that functionality is rarely used. Despite this, I don't think anyone would argue that today's more complex cell phones are bad.

Annuities Create a Tax Time Bomb

Generally speaking, paying taxes later is better than paying taxes now. Therefore, one of the key benefits of an annuity is that it allows your money to grow tax deferred. I cover the benefits of tax deferral in the chapter on taxation, so I won't go into great lengths on it here. However, it is important to point out that tax deferral is not tax free. Someone is going to have to pay the taxes at some point in time. In exchange for allowing annuities to grow tax deferred, the tax code requires that when the income is received, taxes must be paid at ordinary income tax rates. Other assets, if held for more than a year, are typically taxed at the lower (for now) capital gains rate. In addition, if you have deferred the taxes for a long time, the tax bill can indeed be substantial. But the reality is that almost no one, because of the potential taxes, ever takes all the income at once. Typically, the income is received over a number of years, thereby stretching the tax bill out. In addition, the income is most often received after your working years when you are often in a lower tax bracket. The most common exception to this is when a beneficiary receives the value of the annuity upon the death of the person that originally owned it. However, even in these situations the beneficiary always has the option of receiving the money over time. Rarely do they elect to take the money all at once. But even if they choose to do so, I've yet to see a beneficiary complain about receiving the value of an annuity contract simply because he or she must then turn over some of the proceeds to the IRS.

Most people in retirement rely on several buckets of money for their retirement income. In addition to social security and possibly a pension, they might have an IRA, 401(k), a regular investment account, CDs, etc. All these assets can have unique tax impacts. If that sounds like your situation, it's important that you work with a financial professional on how best to coordinate the receipt of the income in a manner that reduces your overall taxes from year to year. Adding an annuity to this mix simply adds another layer of complexity to the best overall withdrawal strategy.

Adding a Tax-Deferred Asset to a Tax-Deferred Account Doesn't Make Sense

Approximately half of the annuities outstanding are held within retirement accounts such as IRAs and 403(b)s. The tax code allows any asset in these accounts to grow tax deferred as a means to encourage us to set aside money for our retirement. It is therefore true that putting an annuity into your IRA, for example, gets you no additional tax advantages. Whether you are buying an annuity, mutual fund, or individual stock or bond, as long as that asset stays in the retirement account, you will pay no taxes on any gains or interest. However, that does not automatically mean that it therefore makes no sense to put an annuity into that retirement plan. It simply means that the investment merits of the annuity itself must be able to stand on their own against the investment merits of any other possible investment. The annuity has no extra advantage due to its inherent tax deferral; therefore, there must be other reasons to choose an annuity. The simplest example is the comparison between a fixed annuity and a bank CD. If your goal is to have some of your retirement dollars in an investment that is guaranteed and will pay a specific amount of interest each year, a bank CD is a common option. But what if a three-year bank CD is paying only 2 percent, but a three-year fixed annuity is paying 3 percent? Both provide a guarantee of your investment (although only the CD comes with FDIC insurance), and both pay a specific rate for three years, after which you have the option of renewing the term. Since they both would sit in your retirement account, both would be tax deferred. Even if you perceive the fixed annuity to be a bit riskier because of the lack of FDIC insurance, you might be willing to take that slight additional risk in order to get the higher rate of return.

The fact that one of them is in the form of an annuity is not in itself a reason to buy or not buy it.

Similarly, a variable annuity might be a better option than a mutual fund because of the guaranteed death benefits and income benefits that they can offer—benefits that mutual funds don't have. But these benefits come with an additional cost as well. The question therefore is, Is the guarantee that your beneficiaries will not get less than you invested upon your death (as an example) worth the additional 1–1.5 percent you will have to pay to get that guarantee? If you're below the age of sixty and therefore have a low probability of death, probably not. However, if you are over eighty, maybe so. The point remains that tax deferral is not an advantage if you buy a variable annuity in a tax-deferred retirement account. Therefore, does the annuity have additional benefits that make it worth the extra cost?

Annuities Are Often Sold Because of Their "High" Commission, Not Because They Are the Best Answer for the Consumer

This argument could be made for any product that is sold for a commission. Any commission-based sale creates a conflict of interest between the salesperson and the client. Since the salesperson only gets paid if you buy, is the salesperson making the recommendation because it's the right one for you or because it's the right one for him or her?

As mentioned above, over 95 percent of the annuities sold today pay a commission to the advisor who is making the recommendation. Since the average annuity purchase is about $125,000 and the typical commission is 5–6 percent, the advisor stands to make $6,000–$7,500 on the average annuity sale. That's not a bad day's work. But is that a reason in itself not to buy an annuity? Not in my opinion. Everything goes back to *what is the need* and *how does the annuity meet that need* versus other options. The typical annuity commission is very similar to the typical real estate commission. While the size of the commission might cause someone to try to sell their house without an agent, no one decides not to buy or sell a house simply because they don't want a real estate agent to receive a commission. It's about the need for the house and the value provided by the agent. Annuities are no different. Is a 5–6 percent commission too high? I'll leave that to you to decide.

My Thoughts

Beware of any advisor who makes annuities the focal point of his or her practice. While specialization can be helpful with a product as diverse and complex as annuities, it also means that advisor believes that annuities are the solution for almost everyone. Similarly, beware of any advisor who holds a disdain for annuities. In my experience, many of those advisors examine annuities only to find the potential flaws of the product. Their predisposition to disregard all annuities as overly costly and complex can often blind them to the benefits annuities can provide.

Focus on the following questions:

- What is the financial problem you are looking to solve?
- How does an annuity solve that problem?
- What does that solution cost you—not only in terms of actual fees but in product restrictions and liquidity?
- Can you live with those trade-offs?

These four questions aren't unique to annuities, of course. These are really the same questions you should ask about any investment you are considering.

These last features give clients even more ability to shore up against the same uncertainties, as I will talk about in the investment and insurance chapters.

ALL ANNUITIES ARE NOT CREATED EQUAL

My shopping list for a recent grocery store visit contained what appeared to be two simple items: Oreos and toothpaste. If you have shopped for either recently, you know where I'm heading. The decision used to be simple—regular Oreos or Double Stuf. No more. Sometime since I last shopped for Oreos, Nabisco decided that we needed sixteen different types of Oreos. I was particularly intrigued by the limited edition Key Lime Pie Oreos. Call me a traditionalist, but that just didn't seem like an Oreo at all. The toothpaste choices seemed even more mystifying. If Crest Complete really lives up to its name, I couldn't help but wonder why I needed any other choices at all. Yet, there are even more toothpaste choices than choices for Oreos. It was obvious to me that whether it be Oreos or toothpaste, one cannot make any general statements about either of them. Annuities are no different.

> **THE REALITY IS THAT, LIKE OREOS AND TOOTHPASTE, ANNUITIES COME IN MANY DIFFERENT SHAPES AND SIZES.**

It is not uncommon to see articles on annuities that make broad, sweeping statements such as, "Annuities Are Too Expensive," or

"Annuities Are Too Complicated." Such statements imply that every annuity, no matter what type, is the same. The reality is that, like Oreos and toothpaste, annuities come in many different shapes and sizes. Therefore, any such general statements are going to be both true and not true. So, let's get started by briefly describing the different types of annuities that are commonly found today. This chapter is designed to allow you to easily recognize the various types of annuities. Subsequent chapters will cover each type of annuity in more detail.

Immediate Annuities

Commonly referred to as single premium immediate annuities, or SPIAs, immediate annuities are the oldest form of annuities. In fact, prior to the 1970s, it was the only form of annuities that insurance companies offered. The word "annuity" comes from the Latin word "annua," which means an annual stipend. The first annuities actually date back to the Roman Empire. Roman citizens would pay into the "annua" in exchange for receiving an annual income for life. Roman soldiers were sometimes promised an income for life in exchange for their service in the army. While today's annuities are much more sophisticated, the concept remains the same. You enter into a contract with an insurance company that promises to pay you a regular income for a specified period of time in exchange for a lump sum deposit. Effectively, you are creating your own pension that starts immediately and is funded with a single payment—hence the name single premium immediate annuity.

There are two great uncertainties when planning for retirement: the rate of return you will achieve on your portfolio and how long you are going to live. Locking in an income for life via an immediate annuity greatly simplifies the planning process. In fact, a growing amount of research has demonstrated that retirement planning becomes significantly more effective when an immediate annuity becomes part of the plan. While all this research is very impressive, I see no need to cite any of it to prove the value of an immediate annuity. All you need to do is find a baby boomer with a pension and another without a pension and ask each of them how financially secure they feel about their retirement. I can pretty much guarantee you that the individual with an income for life in the form of a pension feels far more financially secure than the person who has to worry about what income his or her retirement nest egg will maintain.

Deferred Income Annuities

Deferred income annuities, or DIAs, are a cousin of single premium immediate annuities. At the end of the day, though, DIAs are really just delayed immediate annuities. When you buy a DIA, you agree to give the insurance company a lump sum or a series of deposits over time in exchange for an income for life that begins more than one year from now. Typically, these are bought either by people in their fifties who are anticipating retiring within ten years or by people in their sixties or seventies ho want a stream of income to begin at age eighty or eighty-five to provide them an additional source of income should they live beyond their life expectancy. Many retirees are concerned about excessive healthcare costs late in life. And with good reason. Nothing will blow up a well-designed retirement plan faster than a large, unexpected healthcare cost. Knowing that you have a new source of income that will kick in late in life can bring any retiree tremendous peace of mind.

Fixed Annuities

A fixed annuity is the insurance industry's version of a CD. Like a CD, the insurance company guarantees a specific rate of return for a specified period of time. For example, an insurance company might offer a fixed annuity that guarantees 4.5 percent per year for three years or 5.5 percent for five years. Also like a CD, there is likely to be a cost to get out of the annuity prior to the end of the rate guarantee. There are, however, two big differences. First and foremost, while the insurance company "guarantees" the invested amount and the amount of interest, the guarantee is only as strong as the company itself. They are not FDIC insured. Second, like every other annuity, no taxes are due on the earned interest until it is withdrawn from the annuity. Interest credited to a CD is taxable each year even if you leave the interest at the bank to compound within your account.

Fixed Indexed Annuities

A fixed indexed annuity, or FIA, is another form of a fixed annuity. Both of them guarantee that the value you invest will not decline in value. However, whereas a fixed annuity guarantees a specific rate each year, a fixed indexed annuity provides a return tied to a specific stock index, such as the S&P 500. At the end of the term you select, the insurance company will compare the value of the index to the value on the day you made the investment. If the index has increased in value, you will get a portion of that return. For example, if the index is up 10 percent, you might earn 5–6 percent. However, if the index falls in value, the value of your investment will not fall. You will just earn 0 percent for that particular time period. Since you are trading off the known return of the traditional fixed annuity for an unknown return of a FIA, over the long run, you should expect to earn about

1–1.5 percent more per year on the FIA. But remember, they both guarantee that you won't get a negative return.

Variable Annuities

For the most part of the last twenty years, variable annuities have captured more than half of the roughly $270 billion in annuities that are purchased each year. Not surprisingly, therefore, most of the broad, sweeping statements about annuities are really about this particular product. And I'm sure it also won't surprise you that even when referring to this particular product, those general statements are sometimes true and sometimes not so true. Insurance companies introduced variable annuities back in the 1980s in an attempt to compete with the growing popularity of mutual funds. Essentially, a variable annuity is a pool of mutual funds wrapped into an annuity contract. The insurance company selects a group of money managers to manage a fund or group of funds that are similar to a mutual fund they already manage. For example, many insurance companies hire American Funds, one of the largest money managers, to manage a "growth" account within their variable annuity that looks a lot like the Growth Fund of America mutual fund. By law, the insurance company is not allowed to use the same publicly traded mutual fund in a deferred annuity, so they ask American Funds to construct a similar fund with the same portfolio managers and the same investment objectives. They will make the same request to Vanguard, Fidelity, Franklin-Templeton, etc. At the end, you will have an annuity that allows you to choose between upward of one hundred different stocks, bonds, or alternative investment accounts managed by twenty to thirty different fund managers. In fact, one variable annuity has almost four hundred different investment options.

These are referred to as variable annuities because, unlike the fixed annuities described above, the expected return will be variable each year (proving once again that the insurance industry never has been very good at coming up with catchy names). Unlike mutual funds, however, most variable annuities come with certain guarantees. They might have a guaranteed death benefit that can pay more to your beneficiary than the investment is worth, and/or they might have a guaranteed living benefit that pays you an income for life based on an amount that is greater than the value of the investment. We'll go into these benefits in greater detail in a later chapter. For now, all you need to know is that the claims that variable annuities have higher fees than mutual funds is indeed true. However, many of the additional fees are a result of the unique guarantees provided by the annuity.

Structured Annuities (or Registered Indexed Linked Annuities)

Structured annuities are the newest innovation in the world of annuities. They're basically part variable annuity and part FIA. Like an FIA, the return is tied to a specific index. Depending on the index and time period you select, you might get some, all, or possibly more than the return of the index. But like a variable annuity, if the index goes down in value, the value of your investment can fall with it. The structured annuity is designed to cover a portion of the drop in the index, but not necessarily all of it. One of the nice aspects of structured annuities is that you can decide how much protection you want. The more you select, the less upside you will potentially return.

RISK VERSUS REWARD SUMMARY

If you line the various types of annuities up against each other on the basis of potential return versus protection of your investment, they would compare as follows:

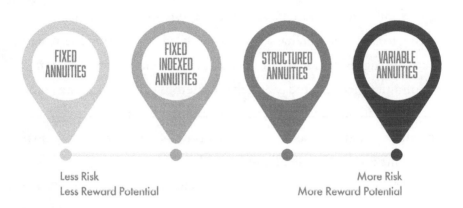

FIXED ANNUITIES   FIXED INDEXED ANNUITIES   STRUCTURED ANNUITIES   VARIABLE ANNUITIES

Less Risk
Less Reward Potential   More Risk
More Reward Potential

Questions to Ask

Fisher Investments has an online post entitled, "Why We Hate Annuities." I would suggest you retain a degree of skepticism anytime you see such a broad, general statement. Odds are the person making such a claim has an agenda. In this case, Fisher Investments wants you to cash in your annuity and move the money to their firm so that they can collect an annual asset charge on your money. So, the next time you hear a financial advisor or any other type of investment "expert" make a sweeping statement about annuities, such as, "Annuities are complex," "Annuities are costly," or even "Annuities are great," ask the following questions:

1. "All annuities, or are you referring to a specific type of annuity? If so, which type?"

2. "What specifically do you not like about annuities?" or, "What specifically do you like about annuities?" And, "Why do you feel that way?"
3. "If I was talking to a person who owns an annuity, what would he or she likely say about it?"
4. "What do I get for the costs?"

If you don't get specific answers to these questions, then you are talking to someone who has a shallow knowledge of annuities. I would therefore suggest you seek out another advisor. Given the broad range of annuities that exist today and the numerous options that can come with them, it's important that you seek out someone who actively uses annuities as part of the retirement income planning process. Those who don't ever recommend annuities likely have a bias against them. Similarly, an advisor who concludes that an annuity is appropriate for almost everyone likely has an opposite bias. You'll be best served by an advisor that has sampled all sixteen different types of Oreos but has not loaded his or her cart up with one or more of each.

Or you could just keep reading this book.

A FEW THINGS ALL ANNUITIES HAVE IN COMMON

Despite all the different types of annuities, there are certain things they all have in common.

Every Annuity Is an Actual Contract Between You and the Insurance Company

In this day and age, I'm not sure why insurance companies still have to issue you an actual contract. I suspect it's more because "that's the way we've always done it" than anything else. When you buy an annuity, you will receive a pretty lengthy document that will cover in detail all the provisions of the policy you purchased. Under state regulations, you will have ten to thirty days to review the contract. This "free look" period begins when you actually receive the document—either directly from the insurance company or from the agent who sold you the policy. If for any reason you change your mind during this period, the insurance company is required to give you a full refund of your money.

No Taxes Are Payable until the Income Is Paid to You

As long as you leave any interest or earnings in the contract to continue to work for you, no 1099 will be sent to you. The industry phrase is "tax deferred" because the taxes will have to eventually be paid. Therefore, you are only deferring them into the future. The beauty of tax deferral is that the money you would have otherwise paid in taxes each year stays in your account to earn additional interest for you. It's like an interest-free loan from Uncle Sam. This is why money grows faster if you can defer your taxes.

When Taxes Are Due, They Are Considered Ordinary Income

Because the government grants tax-deferred status to annuities, it requires that when the interest or earnings are paid to you, they must be reported as ordinary income—just like wages. There is no capital gains treatment, which generally is a much lower tax rate. I will note that if you still own the annuity when you die, the proceeds will be paid to the beneficiary you list on the contract, and any final taxes will be paid by that beneficiary at that person's tax bracket. Unlike other assets, there is no stepped-up cost basis at death.

Annuities Avoid Probate

As long as you name an individual or individuals as the beneficiary of the contract, the proceeds will be paid directly to that beneficiary once the annuity company receives the death certificate and payment instructions. This allows annuities to completely avoid probate. Why is this important? The probate process can take months if not years depending upon the complexity of the estate. Beneficiaries of the estate therefore may have to wait a long time until they get much-needed money. There is no such wait for annuity proceeds. In addition, the cost of probate is based on the size of the estate. Therefore, any asset that avoids the process will save the estate money. And finally, anything that goes through probate becomes a matter of public record, allowing anyone to see what someone has inherited. That is not the case with an annuity.

Every Annuity Must Have Three Different Designations

First, every annuity must have an owner. This is the person who buys the annuity and controls it while it exists. In addition to the owner, there is an "annuitant." The annuitant is the person whose life the income is based on once it begins (if it does begin at all—more on that later). In the vast majority of cases, the owner and the annuitant are the same person. In fact, I rarely suggest that it be any other way. Anytime I've seen someone have a problem with the structure of an annuity, it's almost always because they made the owner and annuitant different people. We'll cover more on that later in the book. Finally, every annuity has to have at least one beneficiary. This is the person(s) that gets the money when the determining owner (typically the annuitant) dies. If there is more than one beneficiary, the owner can designate what percentage each of the beneficiaries receives. The beneficiary can be changed at any time. As an alternative, you have the option of naming your estate as the beneficiary. I do not recommend this option. If you name your estate as the beneficiary, you will not avoid probate upon death. The annuity will simply go into the total estate with any other probated assets.

At Some Point, All Annuities Must Be Turned into an Income Stream (or Not)

The primary purpose of any annuity is to ultimately provide a stream of income in retirement. This is the main reason the federal government provides for them to grow tax deferred until the money is received. Our politicians in Washington, DC, don't want to be financially responsible for our retirement. Therefore, they provide all kinds of incentives for us to save for retirement. Allowing annuities to grow without taxation is one of those incentives. In exchange, they expect you to use that annuity for retirement.

Therefore, every annuity contract will have an age at which you must start taking the money out. This is known as the "maximum annuitization age." On the other hand, insurance companies only make money if you keep assets in the annuity. Therefore, they are in no hurry to force you to take it. Consequently, the maximum annuitization age on most contracts is eighty-five or ninety years old. Some go even longer. This means this provision is rarely important—at least until you start to reach the required age. But even if that happens, I find that most people don't mind getting an extra check in the mail. And by then you are likely to have extra medical expenses.

Summary

Other than these six things, annuities can differ greatly and can help meet many financial goals. Just remember that an annuity is like a Swiss Army knife. While it may be designed to do many things, it typically will only do one or two things really well. Therefore, it's imperative that before you purchase any annuity, you be very clear on what financial goal you want it to achieve. Is it to accumulate money for retirement, provide some protection for your retirement assets, or provide a guaranteed income for life? And if it's the latter, when do you need the income to begin and how much do you need? Taking the time to answer those questions will increase the likelihood that you will match the right annuity with the right financial goal.

THE BEAUTY OF LIFETIME INCOME

When we think about saving for retirement, we often think in terms of setting a goal to accumulate a specific amount of money. In fact, not long ago, ING insurance company (now Voya Financial) used to run ads that asked, "What's your number?" The goal of the ad was to encourage you to calculate how much you think you need to save in order to have enough for a secure retirement. Given that studies have shown that the greatest fear of most retirees is not having enough money to maintain a reasonable standard of living, trying to reach a specific savings goal seems to make sense.

THERE ARE ONLY THREE WAYS TO GET AN INCOME GUARANTEED FOR LIFE—SOCIAL SECURITY, A PENSION, AND AN ANNUITY.

However, when you think about it, it's not about how much you have on the day you retire, but rather how much income you have each year in retirement. The goal, therefore, should be about creating an adequate stream of income that will last as long as you do. Yes, you must first save money in order to create that income, but at the end of the day, what is more important: having $1 million on the day you retire or getting $50,000 per year, every year, for as long as you live?

The fact of the matter is there are only three ways to get an income guaranteed for life—social security, a pension, and an annuity. If either you or your spouse worked at all during your lifetime, you will get a social security benefit. However, in March of 2022, the average social security benefit was only $1,537 per month, or less than $20,000 per year. Good luck living on that. Sadly, according to the Social Security Administration, among elderly social security beneficiaries, 21 percent of married couples and about 45 percent of unmarried persons rely on social security for 90 percent or more of their income. The truth of the matter is that social security was never designed to be the primary source of retirement income. It was and still is meant to simply supplement retirement income, and at least make sure everyone has some income in retirement.

Fortunately, many retirees today are collecting a pension in addition to social security. The combination of the two can make a very financially secure retirement. However, today pensions exist almost solely in the public sector. If you don't work for the government, you likely don't have a pension available to you. Increasingly, people reaching retirement today need to fund their own retirement.

If you don't have a pension and want more guaranteed lifetime income than social security will pay, that leaves only one option—an annuity. Every financial planner will run a financial plan that will give you the probability that your retirement assets will sustain you through retirement. Typically, these plans shoot for an 85–90 percent probability that you will both be able to cover your essential expenses and not run out of money before you die. That sounds pretty safe, right? However, there is one major problem with this calculation. It is always based on assumed age at death—typically eighty-five or ninety.

What this is really telling you is that as long as you die by that assumed age, there is an 85–90 percent probability that you will not run out of money. But that also means there is a 10–15 percent chance that you will not have an adequate income throughout retirement. Are you willing to take that chance? And what if you live longer than that? What if you live to one hundred? Change the assumptions to that age, and you will undoubtedly find that your probability of running out of money increases significantly. While centurions are still relatively rare, medical advances are making them more and more common every year. Do you really want to bet on the possibility that you will die at the age assumed in the financial plan? In my mind, this is one of those bets where the consequences of losing are too great to take. Therefore, my retirement plan includes funding enough annuities to provide me enough guaranteed income to live comfortably, no matter how long I live.

Despite Common Wisdom, Guaranteed Lifetime Income Actually Gives You More Investment Flexibility

Most financial advisors avoid annuities as part of a retirement income plan because they believe that locking up a significant portion of your retirement assets within an annuity eliminates investment flexibility. It is true that to provide sufficient retirement income, you likely have to utilize a substantial amount of your total retirement income savings. A sixty-five-year-old male who wants $50,000 per year for life will likely have to put about $900,000 into an annuity to generate that amount of income. I completely get how tough it is to take that much of the money you worked so hard to save and send it to an insurance company. However, once you accept this trade-off, think of the flexibility you have with the rest of your retirement savings. The reality is that if you don't purchase a guaranteed income for life, your financial advisor is going to have to invest your money much more conservatively than they otherwise would, simply to protect you from a significant stock market decline.

If you have saved enough for retirement, a 5–20 percent decline in stocks is not going to have a meaningful impact on your results. Such declines occur every couple of years and typically recover very quickly. It's the 30–50 percent decline that occurs every ten years or so that will destroy even the best retirement plan—especially if that happens not long after you retire.

The fact of the matter is that your likelihood of success (once you retire) is, to a great extent, mostly about timing. If you retire while stocks are beginning a steady, multiyear climb, you will have nothing to worry about. Think of it as having the wind at your back. If, on the other hand, you retired in 2000 or 2007, the beginning of the last two major bear markets, any retirement plan you put in place, no matter how good it was, was shot completely to hell—unless you had purchased an annuity. If your retirement income is both guaranteed for life and thereby protected from the ups and downs of the market, you don't need to change the rest of your investments one bit. More importantly, you likely won't need to make any changes to your lifestyle as well. You won't have to reconsider that dream vacation simply because the stock market "plunged" (as the papers like to call it). In fact, you can take advantage of the market decline by allocating more money to stocks so that you can take advantage of the inevitable rebound.

So Why Don't More People Buy an Annuity for Guaranteed Lifetime Income?

Twenty-five years ago I listened to a very compelling presentation by Dick Austin, one of the founding fathers of the annuity industry, about the upcoming need that baby boomers and subsequent generations were going to have for guaranteed lifetime income. Faced with longer lives and no pension, Mr. Austin concluded that people would buy annuities in mass quantities. It all made perfect sense to most of those listening. There's only one problem. The demand for those annuities never materialized. Yes, over $250 billion in annuities are bought each year. But that's dwarfed by the trillions of dollars invested each year in mutual funds and CDs. And of those that do buy an annuity, a good chunk buy them for reasons other than securing a guaranteed income for life. I offer three explanations as to why the prediction from twenty-five years ago never came true.

EVERYONE WANTS A PENSION, BUT FEW WANT TO FUND IT WITH THEIR OWN MONEY

Buying an annuity to provide an income for life—either beginning immediately or at some time in the future—is essentially like purchasing your own pension. You give the insurance company some of your money, and in exchange the insurance company agrees to pay you an income for as long as you live, or if you prefer, as long as you and your spouse live. Sounds like a pension, right? But here's the problem. If someone is lucky enough to have a pension, they never really feel like they funded it out of their own pocket. Intuitively they understand that they received less in take-home pay in exchange for having a pension plan at work. However, there is no line item on a pay stub that says how much money was deducted in order to fund that pension. Therefore, the pensioner never saw the money. And they certainly never wrote a large check to the company paying the pension. Social security isn't much different. While we see the money that is deducted from each paycheck for FICA, it's not like we have a choice in the matter. It's not money we can get, so we don't really look at it as if we are buying our future social security benefit.

It becomes a whole different ball game when you have to make a conscious decision to hand over a chunk of your hard-earned savings to some insurance company. If I managed to save $500,000 for retirement over the years, and I'm told I need to write a $200,000 check to the insurance company in order to get $12,000 per year in lifetime income, that check becomes very difficult to write. No one wants to see their $500,000 in savings drop by 40 percent overnight—even if they know they will get an income in return. And that brings us to the second problem.

MOST PEOPLE UNDERVALUE AN INCOME FOR LIFE

Quick question: How much do you think $1,537 per month in income for life—the average monthly social security benefit—is worth in a lump sum for a sixty-five-year-old? In other words, if the federal government gave you the option at age sixty-five to get a lump sum check instead of getting a social security benefit, how much should they give you? Would you be surprised to learn that they should have to give you more than $300,000? And that ignores the spousal benefit that comes with social security. Studies have shown that if you ask someone how much an annual income for life that $100,000 should be able to buy, they typically overestimate the actual amount of income by 20–40 percent. The fact of the matter is that it costs a lot to fund an income for life—especially at today's relatively low interest rates.

MANY FINANCIAL ADVISORS THINK A GUARANTEED INCOME FOR LIFE IS SIMPLY NOT NECESSARY

Many financial advisors get paid an ongoing fee on assets in order to make investment decisions and recommendations on your behalf. Their financial planning software will tell them the return they must earn on your assets in order to give you that 85–90 percent probability of providing the income you need in retirement without having to significantly reduce your lifestyle. They will carefully put together a plan that will achieve this return. If they are doing their job, they will periodically review your progress against this plan and recommend changes when necessary in order to keep you on track. If everything goes as planned, then you won't need an annuity. But remember, unless you have so much money that a plan really isn't even necessary, no plan can guarantee you won't have to eventually choose between reducing your lifestyle or running out of money before you die. Too much is unknown, starting with how long you will live. In addition, the plan will have to make assumptions about market returns and interest rates. Those assumptions will most certainly be wrong. The errors could be in your favor—for example, the stock market might return more than expected—or the errors might go against you. So why not just recommend an annuity and lock in that desired income, and then just invest the money that is not used to fund the annuity? Think about it. If you are paying me for my investment expertise, it's hard for me to recommend that you use some of your money to buy an annuity because I might not be right. You didn't pay me to essentially outsource part of the investment process to an insurance company. Or did you? Didn't you pay me to make sure that you will have a financially secure retirement ? Do you really care if an annuity is part of the solution as long as the solution works? I don't think so. However, not every financial advisor would view it that way.

IN SUMMARY

I've been in the financial services industry since 1983. I like to think I know what I'm doing. I certainly know more than the average person when it comes to investing money. However, I can assure you that I have already established the means to provide myself a significant amount of income guaranteed for life from two different annuities. I've done this for two reasons. First and foremost, I don't want to worry about it. Once I retire, I don't want to have to check how the market did that day (or week or month or year) and what that might mean for my ability to generate income from my portfolio down the road. I want to know that check is going to show up each month no matter what. Second, I've come to realize that no matter how much you know about investments, you sometimes just get it wrong. Either you didn't see the pandemic coming, or you overestimated the market impact or underestimated how quickly the market would recover. Take your pick. The fact of the matter is that stuff happens. Which brings me back to my first reason. I don't want to have to worry about stuff happening. And what if I live to be one hundred? I don't want to have to worry about that either. Do you?

Sequence of Returns: No Big Deal While You Are Saving, but a Very Big Deal When You Start Taking Income

Sequence of returns refers to the order in which you earn a return on your money. As an example, the following table lists the returns for the S&P 500 for each year since 2006. This would be considered the sequence of returns for the S&P 500 for each of the last fifteen years.

YEAR	S&P 500 RETURN	YEAR	S&P 500 RETURN
2006	15.79%	2014	13.69%
2007	5.49%	2015	1.38%
2008	-37.00%	2016	11.96%
2009	26.46%	2017	21.83%
2010	15.06%	2018	-4.38%
2011	2.11%	2019	31.49%
2012	16.00%	2020	18.40%
2013	32.39%		

Had you invested $100,000 in the S&P 500 at the beginning of 2006 and never touched the investment, even during the dark days of 2007–2009, you would have $410,928 by the end of 2020. This calculates out to an average rate of return of 9.98 percent, which is actually pretty close to the stock market's historical average return. As a side note, you will notice the extremely wide range of annual outcomes—from a negative 37 percent in 2008 offset by two years that returned more than 30 percent. You will also note that the market experienced only two down years over this fifteen-year period as compared to the three to four one would expect given that the market typically goes down every one in four years. The point is that while the stock market provides good long-term results, no one really knows what the next twelve to twenty-four months will bring.

Let's assume for a minute that the order of these returns is reversed. Rather than 15.79 percent in the first year followed by 5.49 percent, we get 18.40 percent in the first year followed by 31.49 percent (the returns for 2020 and 2019), and so on. Would the change in the sequence of returns change our total return over this fifteen-year time period? The answer is no. As long as the money is left alone to grow, the order or sequence of the returns doesn't matter at all. We will always end up with the same amount of money.

But is this also true if the money is touched? For example, what if I'm taking $5,000 per year from my account in order to supplement my retirement income? Does the sequence of returns matter then? The answer is most definitely yes. Poor returns early in retirement can have a dramatic impact on your likelihood to run out of money. Conversely, good returns early in retirement greatly improve the probability that you will not only not run out of money but will also have plenty more money to spend.

Let's look at a very simple example. Let's assume that Mrs. Saver has set aside $500,000 for retirement and elects to take out 5 percent, or $25,000, per year each year. Mrs. Saver's returns over her first 10 years of retirement are 10 percent, 15 percent, 5 percent, 10 percent, 5 percent, -10 percent, -15 percent, 20 percent, 10 percent, and 5 percent—in that order. How much money would Mrs. Saver have in her account after ten years, assuming she took out $25,000 each year?

YEAR	ACCOUNT VALUE	RETURN	ACCOUNT VALUE AFTER RETURN	WITHDRAWAL	ACCOUNT VALUE AT YEAR END
1	$500,000	10%	$550,000	$25,000	$525,000
2	$525,000	15%	$603,750	$25,000	$578,750
3	$578,750	5%	$607,688	$25,000	$582,688
4	$582,688	10%	$640,956	$25,000	$615,956
5	$615,956	5%	$646,754	$25,000	$621,754
6	$621,754	-10%	$559,579	$25,000	$534,579
7	$534,579	-15%	$454,392	$25,000	$429,392
8	$429,392	20%	$515,270	$25,000	$490,270
9	$490,270	10%	$539,297	$25,000	$514,297
10	$514,297	5%	$540,012	$25,000	$515,012

We can see that Mrs. Saver, even after taking $25,000 per year for ten years, has more money after the tenth year than she started with. Her returns more than offset her total withdrawals of $250,000. More importantly, the order or sequence of her returns helped.

Now let's look at Mrs. Saver's brother, Mr. Saver. He, too, managed to save $500,000 for retirement, but he chose to retire six years after his sister—just before the market returned -10 percent and then -15 percent. In the other years, we'll assume he received the identical annual returns. We're just changing the order, starting with the two negative years and then moving to 20 percent, 10 percent, 5 percent, and then back to the top of the above chart to 10 percent, 15 percent, etc. What was his experience?

YEAR	ACCOUNT VALUE	RETURN	ACCOUNT VALUE AFTER RETURN	WITHDRAWAL	ACCOUNT VALUE AT YEAR END
1	$500,000	-10%	$450,000	$25,000	$425,000
2	$425,000	-15%	$361,250	$25,000	$336,250
3	$336,250	20%	$403,500	$25,000	$378,500
4	$378,500	10%	$416,350	$25,000	$391,350
5	$391,350	5%	$410,918	$25,000	$385,918
6	$385,918	10%	$424,509	$25,000	$399,509
7	$399,509	15%	$459,436	$25,000	$434,436
8	$434,436	5%	$456,157	$25,000	$431,157
9	$431,157	10%	$474,273	$25,000	$449,273
10	$449,273	5%	$471,737	$25,000	$446,737

His remaining account balance after ten years is only $446,737, 13 percent less than his sister. The notable thing here is that they both did exactly the same thing. They both saved the same amount of money and took out the same amount of money. The only difference was pure, dumb luck. Mrs. Saver had the good fortune of retiring just before the market went up for five straight years, while her brother had the misfortune of retiring just before the market dropped for two straight years. The only difference was the sequence of the returns they both experienced. Now Mr. Saver may need to consider cutting back his withdrawal rate in order to make sure he doesn't run out of money, while his sister could actually begin to increase her withdrawal rate if she wanted to.

Actually, the numbers used in this example are not very extreme. Think about the same story, but one of the Savers retiring in 2007, just before the market declined 37 percent, while the other retired in 2009, just before the market went on a nine-year winning streak. How different would their experience be then?

Why Am I Bringing This Up in a Book on Annuities?

When you are planning for retirement, there are really only two things you can control—the amount you are saving toward retirement and the amount of income you elect to take from your retirement portfolio each year. Many think they can also control when they retire, but that's not always the case. Unfortunately, there are many out there who were forced to retire before they planned—either for health reasons or because their company decided they no longer needed them. Even if you are one of the lucky ones who can control your retirement date, there are three things no one can control:

1. The date you will die—in other words, the length of your retirement, which is known as longevity risk
2. The returns your retirement savings will get each year
3. The sequence of those returns

The goal, therefore, is to manage the risks associated with these three things. While an annuity cannot help with the second of these three risks, it can most certainly help with the other two. Providing an income that you can't outlive helps reduce longevity risk. It doesn't guarantee that you will have as much income as you always want, but it does guarantee an income beyond what social security provides.

Using an annuity to provide an income for life also reduces your sequence of returns risk. The amount of income provided by the annuity, unlike the rest of your retirement income portfolio, is not impacted in any way by the year-to-year returns of the stock market. Since a significant drop in the market in your first year or two of retirement does not alter your annuity income **THE ANNUITY PUTS TIME ON YOUR SIDE.** in any way; you don't have to make any hard decisions about either changing your portfolio or altering your withdrawal rate. You can leave your portfolio fully invested, wait for the market to go back up, and put your portfolio back to your assumed path. The annuity puts time on your side.

Ask your advisor which client is easier to manage in retirement—one with a pension or one without a pension. He or she will most certainly tell you that it's significantly easier to manage retirement for the person who has both a pension and social security than the person with just social security. The additional guaranteed income for life provided by the pension allows the advisor to be more flexible and less conservative with the rest of the portfolio since he or she does not have to worry nearly as much about the impact of the sequence of returns. The annuity gives you the option of creating your own pension.

I've thrown out a lot of new concepts here—sequence of returns, longevity risk, and the potential impact of market volatility on a retirement plan. Let's just break it down to two simple questions. Would you feel more secure in retirement if you had just the $20,000–$25,000 per year that social security pays most people, or would you feel better if you had that, plus another $50,000 paid to you each year in the form of a pension and/or annuity? And which of those two scenarios will allow you to worry less about how the value of your remaining assets fluctuates from day to day or month to month?

HOW ANNUITIES ARE TAXED

In order to protect myself, I'm going to preface this chapter with the statement that I am not a tax attorney, and therefore the information in this chapter should not be considered tax advice. This is merely my understanding of how annuities are taxed based on my forty years in the annuity industry. Please consult a tax expert before making any decisions that could impact your personal tax situation. Now, having gotten that disclaimer out of the way, let's address the topic at hand.

Annuities held in a retirement plan such as an IRA are always taxed according to the rules of that particular retirement plan. There is nothing unique to the taxation simply because the asset within the retirement plan is an annuity. Therefore, this chapter will focus solely on how an annuity is taxed if you own it outside of a retirement account (a nonqualified account).

Taxation Due to a Withdrawal from the Contract

All annuities are taxed as ordinary income when the tax-deferred earnings/interest are paid out to you. Despite the likelihood that you will own the annuity for many years, there is no long-term capital gains treatment. Therefore, when you finally pay the income taxes, you are likely to pay taxes at a higher rate than many other investments. In addition, other assets receive what is called a no stepped-up cost basis at death—meaning any untaxed gains on that asset are cancelled upon your death. This concept was first originated to make sure beneficiaries didn't have to sell the family farm or business in order to pay taxes upon the death of the owner of that farm or business. Unlike most other forms of investments, annuities do not receive this same tax treatment. Your beneficiaries will have to pay taxes on the deferred earnings/interest if you still own the annuity when you die. In short, eventually someone is going to have to pay the taxes, and when it's paid, it will be paid at ordinary income tax rates. This is the trade-off Congress set in exchange for tax-deferred treatment. It's the price you pay in order to not have to pay taxes while the money remains in the annuity. In addition, annuities are taxed based on an accounting concept known as last in, first out (LIFO). Simply put, this means that the earnings/interest, which are added to the contract last, must come out first. For example, if you put $10,000 in an annuity and get interest of $2,000, the first $2,000 you take out is considered income and is therefore taxable. If, on the other hand you take out $3,000, you would report $2,000 in income and get $1,000 of your original investment back.

It's important to understand that all taxable income is the responsibility of the owner, even if the income is paid to someone other than the owner. For example, if you direct the insurance company to pay out the interest to one of your kids in order to help them make a down payment on a house, the tax liability does not shift to them as the recipient of the money. Similarly, you can't avoid the taxes by making the payments payable to a charity (although you will get a charitable deduction for the amount of the contribution).

An Annuity Can Create a Taxable Loss

If you buy an annuity and you ultimately get back less than you invested, you are entitled to report the loss as a deduction against ordinary income. However, the tax code is not clear as to where you should claim the loss on Form 1040. The most conservative approach is to treat it as a miscellaneous itemized deduction not subject to the 2 percent of the adjusted gross income floor. A more aggressive approach is to take the loss under the "other gains or losses" section of the 1040. Given the uncertainty of the policy, you should obviously consult your tax advisor. Fortunately, a loss on an annuity is a pretty rare event. Typically, a loss on annuity is only likely to occur on a variable annuity

FORTUNATELY, A LOSS ON AN ANNUITY IS A PRETTY RARE EVENT.

since this is the only annuity that lets you invest directly in stock and bond funds (subaccounts). While stock and bond funds rise over time, if you were to have a need to cash out the variable annuity not long after purchase, you could most certainly experience a loss. This could also occur with a structured annuity, but the downside protection provided by the contract structure should keep this from being a frequent occurrence. With a fixed or indexed annuity, the only way a loss should ever be incurred is if you cash in the policy shortly after it's purchased, thereby triggering a surrender charge and/or market value adjustment to be greater than the credited interest at the time of the withdrawal.

Exchanging One Annuity for Another— Otherwise Known as a 1035 Exchange

If you are worried about being locked into one specific annuity forever in order to avoid paying taxes, the tax code offers you an out. You are allowed to exchange one annuity for another without creating a taxable event. Essentially, the new annuity inherits the tax situation of the previous annuity. The provision for this tax benefit can be found in Section 1035 of the tax code. Hence the industry has cleverly deemed these annuity exchanges to be a "1035 exchange." However, there are some requirements to comply with the exchange provision. The most important one is that the proceeds of the old annuity must be sent directly to the new annuity company. If you have the money sent to you and you then cash the check, you can't then turn around and send the proceeds on to the new annuity company. By cashing the check, you have taken constructive receipt and therefore created a taxable event.

Taxes upon the Death of the "Holder"

The tax code requires the beneficiary to choose from predetermined distribution options upon the "death of the holder" of the annuity. Unfortunately, the tax code does not define who the "holder" is—although it is presumed to be the owner. The tax code also seems to presume that the owner and the annuitant are always the same, because there is no language as to what must happen if the annuitant and the owner are two different people and the annuitant dies prior to the owner. This ambiguity has caused more than a few tax problems for poorly structured annuity contracts and death benefit decisions that are made without understanding the requirements of this rule. In order to avoid these potential problems, I always advise that you be both the owner and the annuitant on any annuity you buy outside of a retirement plan.

The tax code states that when the holder dies, a spousal beneficiary has four options and a non-spousal beneficiary has three options.

Spousal beneficiary options:

1. Continue the contract as the new owner of the contract. This is the same concept as the spouse taking the ownership of a deceased spouse's IRA. The spouse would simply become the new owner and would name a new beneficiary. All terms of the existing contract continue as before.
2. Receive the death benefit as a lump sum.
3. Elect to annuitize the contract within one year of the date of death.
4. Continue the contract for up to five years. All proceeds of the annuity must be distributed by the fifth anniversary of the death of the holder.

Prior to choosing between these four options, it's essential that the spouse understand how the annuity company interprets the first option. Many annuities—especially variable annuities—can offer guarantees that can cause the value at death to be greater than the actual account value. In these cases, the question becomes, Will the insurance company allow the spouse to continue the contract at the current account value or at the higher death benefit value? A strict interpretation of the tax code would say that the death benefit is the appropriate value only if the beneficiary elects options two, three, or four. I would argue that under the first option, there is no death benefit. It is merely a continuation of the existing contract. Therefore, the death benefit would not be paid until the second spouse dies. Despite this, many insurance companies do allow the spouse to continue the contract at the death benefit value rather than the account value. They do this in order to hold onto the money. If your contract value is $100,000 and your death benefit is $150,000 and the only way you can get the full $150,000 is to take a lump sum or take it over five years, you are going to take the $150,000. Understanding this, some insurance companies will allow the spouse to both take over the contract and increase the account value from $100,000 to the $150,000 death benefit value. It is absolutely critical to check on how the insurance company will treat the death benefit and report the taxes before selecting any option.

Non-spousal beneficiary options:

1. Take a lump sum.
2. Annuitize within twelve months of the date of death.
3. Continue the contract for up to five years.

In short, the non-spouse has the same options of the spouse, with the exception of continuing the contract beyond five years. All these options would be based on the death benefit value rather than the account value. The ability to continue the contract for up to five years is designed as a way to allow the beneficiary to spread the taxes out.

WHO IS RESPONSIBLE FOR PAYING THE TAXES ON THE DEATH BENEFIT?

While determining the correct tax treatment on annuity income is not always a simple task, determining who should pay the taxes is easy. The person receiving the funds must report all the tax-deferred gains paid out by the death benefit. The income is considered ordinary income and is taxed at the recipient's tax bracket.

CAN YOU 1035-EXCHANGE A DEATH BENEFIT IN ORDER TO POSTPONE THE TAXES?

If the beneficiary has no immediate need for the money and doesn't want to avoid reporting the deferred income, it's not uncommon for her to ask if there is a way to continue to defer the taxes by moving the death benefit into another annuity. Unfortunately, that is not possible. The entire objective of creating the death-at-distribution rules was to keep people from deferring taxes through multiple generations.

The bottom line is that if the beneficiary instructs the insurance company to send the death proceeds directly to another insurance company, expect the original insurance company to send the beneficiary a 1099.

WHAT IF A CORPORATION OR TRUST OWNS THE ANNUITY?

The tax deferral afforded to annuities is only available on contracts owned by individuals. A corporation can own an annuity, but it will receive a 1099 for the income (or loss) each year. A trust can also own an annuity. If that trust is established on behalf of an individual, then it's deemed to be owned by that individual and therefore will be tax deferred. Expect the insurance company to request a copy of the trust so that it can determine the appropriate tax treatment. While it's not uncommon to see annuities within trusts, such a structure can create a unique problem at death. Only an individual has the death-benefit options listed above. Since a trust is not an individual, the only option upon the death of the annuitant will be a lump sum payable to the trust.

> WHILE IT'S NOT UNCOMMON TO SEE ANNUITIES WITHIN TRUSTS, SUCH A STRUCTURE CAN CREATE A UNIQUE PROBLEM AT DEATH.

Tax Treatment of Annuitized Policies

This is covered in sufficient detail in the chapter on annuitization. For the purposes of this chapter, I will merely say that when an annuity outside of a retirement plan is annuitized, each income payment is part principal and part interest, based on the life expectancy of the annuitant. The portion of the payment that is nontaxable as a return of premium is called the exclusion allowance and is not taxable. If the annuity payments last long enough to pay out all the cost basis, then 100 percent of the remaining payments become taxable as long as they continue to be paid.

FIXED ANNUITIES

What Are They, and How Can They Protect Your Portfolio?

In their simplest form, fixed annuities are the insurance industry's version of a CD. When you buy a CD from a bank, you give the bank money for a specific period of time and the bank pays you interest on that money each year. In addition, the bank guarantees that you will get all your money back at maturity. However, they typically carry a penalty if you cash the CD out early. The bank then takes the money you gave them and either invests it or lends it out to others with the goal of making more than what they are paying you. In financial terms, the difference between what the bank pays you and what it earns on your money is called a "spread."

YOU GIVE YOUR MONEY TO AN INSURANCE COMPANY. IN RETURN, THE INSURANCE COMPANY WILL GUARANTEE A SPECIFIC RATE OF RETURN FOR ONE TO SEVEN YEARS.

Fixed annuities work much the same way. You give your money to an insurance company. In return, the insurance company will guarantee a specific rate of return for one to seven years. Typically, you can get 10 percent of your fixed annuity value each year should you need to access some of your money. Anything beyond that will carry an early withdrawal penalty like a CD. In the annuity world, this is called a "surrender charge."

There are a few key differences between fixed annuities and CDs:

1. Bank CDs are FDIC insured, while fixed annuities are guaranteed only by the issuing insurance company. However, each state has a state guarantee fund that can reimburse life insurance and annuity policyholders for any losses. The amount of this insurance depends on the state in which you reside but is typically from $100,000 to $300,000 per person per insurance company.

2. Fixed annuities are typically held for a much longer duration than CDs. While CDs can be bought in maturities of five years or more, the vast majority of all CDs purchased carry a maturity of two years or less. Fixed annuities, on the other hand, are designed to be held for three to ten years.

3. Because fixed annuities are a longer time commitment than CDs, they typically pay 1–1.5 percent more in interest than CDs.

4. The interest credited to a CD each year is taxable as ordinary income in that particular year, even if you chose to leave the interest in the CD to earn additional interest for you. This is not the case with annuities. Annuities are tax deferred, which means you don't pay income on the interest credited until you elect to receive it.

5. Unlike CDs, fixed annuities don't actually mature. While they have a period of time during which there is an early withdrawal charge (typically three to ten years), you can cash

in your annuity at any time. In addition, you can leave your money in the annuity even after the early withdrawal period ends. The bottom line is that the insurance company will keep your money and continue to pay interest on your fixed annuity until you tell them you want it or until you die.

Types of Fixed Annuities

Fixed annuities typically fall into one of two categories—annuities that credit interest one year at a time and can change the rate each year, and annuities that guarantee a specific interest rate for the entire length of the early withdrawal period.

TRADITIONAL ANNUITIES THAT GUARANTEE A RATE ONE YEAR AT A TIME

The first fixed annuities that were introduced in the early 1980s guaranteed rates one year at a time. This design continues to this day. Typically, this one-year rate will be about 1.5 percent higher than a one-year CD. But there is a trade-off. While your rate is only good for one year, the contract will have an early withdrawal fee (that "surrender charge") for seven to ten years. That means you have to trust that the insurance company will give you a fair renewal rate at the end of each one-year period. The idea is that the insurance company will pay you a higher rate if rates go up and a lower rate if rates go down. However, it probably won't surprise you to learn that as interest rates in general change, insurance companies tend to be much faster to reduce your rate when rates fall than they are to increase your rate when rates rise.

If you buy a fixed annuity with this design, it's very important that you first get a copy of the history of the insurance company's renewal rates. Most companies try to offer a fair rate of return relative to what they themselves can earn on your money. But it can be tempting for a company to attract your money with an attractive first-year rate and then take advantage of the fact that you can't get out without paying a fee by paying you a below-market rate of return in later years.

MULTIYEAR GUARANTEED ANNUITIES

In response to concerns about what future renewal rates would be, the industry introduced fixed annuities that guarantee a rate for the length of the early withdrawal period. These contracts typically come in three-, five-, and seven-year terms. Within the industry, these are referred to as multiyear guaranteed annuities, or MYGAs for short (the insurance industry loves its acronyms). These contracts are as simple as they get. If you put $100,000 in a three-year fixed annuity paying 4.5 percent for each of the three years, you know that at the end of the three-year period, you will have exactly $114,116. At that point, you can either elect to renew the rate guarantee, move the money to another annuity, or cash in the contract and receive your money.

Remember, however, that annuities, unlike CDs, don't actually mature. Should you elect to leave your money in the existing annuity, one of two things could occur. First, some companies will automatically move you into a new three-year period and restart the three-year early withdrawal charge period. Essentially, this option renews you into a new period within your existing contract. Other companies will give you a new rate that is good for only one year. In these cases, they will not start the early withdrawal charge over again. Since you have completed the initial early withdrawal period, you essentially have an account that you can access anytime you want at no cost. Because you have the flexibility to ask for your money at any time, the insurance company is going to pay you a lower rate of interest than the design that pays a new three-year rate and starts a new three-year charge.

Market Value Adjustments and How They Can Impact Your Annuity Value

If you buy a MYGA, your rate guarantee will most likely come with a market value adjustment (MVA) that will be assessed if you liquidate the annuity prior to the end of an interest rate guarantee. An MVA is in addition to any early withdrawal penalty. This MVA exists to protect the insurance company against an increase in interest rates.

Let me explain. Let's say two years ago when rates were lower, you bought a five-year MVA with a rate guarantee of 2.5 percent. Today, a new contract is paying 5 percent for five years, so you are willing to cash in your annuity early in order to get the higher rate. Or maybe you just need the money, so you elect to cash in the annuity early. In order to give you your money, the insurance company must sell the bonds that they bought with the money you gave them. However, when interest rates rise, the price of those bonds will fall, which means the insurance company is going to take a loss on the bonds when they sell them.

To guard against a drop in the value of the bonds it owns, the insurance company will assess an MVA in addition to any early with-drawal penalty. This MVA will be in the form of a pretty complicated mathematical calculation. This formula will be laid out in the contract you receive. However, there is really only one concept you need to understand. If interest rates have increased since you bought your annuity, the MVA will further reduce the value of the annuity you receive. On the other hand, if interest rates have fallen, the MVA will actually increase the value you will receive. When rates fall, the price of the bonds the insurance company bought using your money will go up. Therefore, the insurance company is willing to share this unexpected gain with you. In fact, as interest rates fell during the early part of the century, many MYGA policyowners elected to cash in their existing annuities in order to get the additional return generated by the MVA. This MVA calculation does not exist to make more profits for the insurance company. It exists only to protect the insurance company from the risk that you get out early and the value of their investments have fallen because of a change in interest rates.

It's also important to note that this MVA calculation is only assessed if you get out of the contract before the end of the period you selected. If you selected a five-year period and you cash in the annuity on your five-year anniversary, no adjustment will be assessed.

Be Wary of "Bonus" Fixed Annuities

In order to help entice you to purchase an annuity, some fixed annuities add a bonus to your investment at the time the annuity is purchased. For example, if you invest $100,000, the insurance company might add $5,000 or even $10,000 to your annuity when the policy is issued. Sounds good, right? Who doesn't want extra money? However, common sense tells you there must be a catch. After all, insurance companies are not in the habit of just giving away money. If the insurance company is going to give you a bonus on your contract, one or more of the following three things will occur:

1. You are going to get a much lower renewal rate than you would get on a contract that does not pay a bonus. In this design, the insurance company is essentially fronting you the interest that they expect to pay over the life of the contract.

2. You are going to have much a much longer early withdrawal period and the cost of getting out early is going to be much higher. To afford the upfront bonus, the insurance company needs more time to recover that bonus. Therefore, you might have an early withdrawal fee for ten or even fifteen years. In addition, bonus annuities typically require that if you choose to get out before that time period, they have to recover much of the bonus they gave you, so they are going to charge you more to get out of the contract early. In short, the surrender charge (early withdrawal fee) will be higher.

3. You could have a vesting period for the bonus. This is a variation of the previous point. Essentially, they credit the bonus upfront, but you are entitled to keep all of it only if you are in the contract for a specific time period—usually ten years. If you get out after one year, you get only 10 percent of the bonus. If you get out after two years, you get only 20 percent of the bonus, and so on.

Bonus annuities are not necessarily a bad choice. In fact, if you plan to stay in the annuity for ten years or more, it may very well pay you more interest than fixed annuities without a bonus. However, it's essential that you understand what you have to give up in exchange for the bonus.

Who Should Buy a Fixed Annuity?

Fixed annuities are an appropriate choice for anyone who wants to know that their account value will grow in value each year and never go down in value from year to year. Because they typically pay more interest than a bank CD and you don't have to pay taxes until you take the money out, they can be a great alternative provided you are

OK with the longer holding period. While you can cash in any annuity at any time, the early withdrawal fees that come with the vast majority of annuities mean that you have to be comfortable with the fact that

THE BOTTOM LINE IS THAT YOU ARE NOT GOING TO GET RICH BUYING A FIXED ANNUITY, BUT YOU'RE NOT GOING TO BECOME POOR EITHER. AND THAT'S PRETTY MUCH THE ENTIRE POINT OF THE PRODUCT.

you are tying up your money for three to ten years, depending upon the design of the annuity. In addition, because of the tax penalty on withdrawals prior to age fifty-nine-and-a-half for annuities purchased outside of retirement plans, annuities are most appropriate for people who are sixty and older. That doesn't mean someone younger than sixty shouldn't buy an annuity. It just means that either a) they are very sure they are not going to need the money prior to reaching fifty-nine-and-a-half or b) that they buy the annuity in a qualified retirement plan such as an IRA.

The bottom line is that you are not going to get rich buying a fixed annuity, but you're not going to become poor either. And that's pretty much the entire point of the product.

INDEXED ANNUITIES

Before I go into what fixed indexed annuities are, let's start with what they are not. An indexed annuity is not an equity investment in any way and should never be represented as an alternative to stocks or mutual funds.

In its simplest form, a fixed indexed annuity is a fixed annuity that does not have a declared interest rate for the upcoming year or more. Instead, the insurance company promises to pay you a return based on the change in price in a particular stock index—normally the S&P 500 index. In this sense, the statement that an indexed annuity gives you a return based on the performance of the stock market is true.

LIKE A FIXED ANNUITY, YOU CAN'T LOSE MONEY ON AN INDEXED ANNUITY.

However, also like a fixed annuity, you can't lose money on an indexed annuity. If the index goes down in value, you simply earn no interest during that year. Just think of this logically. If the insurance company is going to guarantee that you can't lose money, can they really also give you the entire upside of the stock market? Of course not. If they could, this would be the only investment anyone needs. There are various methods for calculating the return you earn, but all of them will give you only a portion of any positive change in the index.

Given the uncertainty of what you will earn on an indexed annuity from year to year, why would someone buy an indexed annuity over a traditional fixed annuity? Over the long run, historically, indexed annuities have averaged 1–1.5 percent more per year than comparable fixed annuities. Therefore, if you are OK with not knowing exactly what you will get for a return each year, and you are OK with occasionally getting no return at all for a year, then an indexed annuity is a great alternative for someone who wants to earn a bit more than more traditional, safe investments, but still have the peace of mind of knowing that their account value will never drop in value.

The Most Commonly Used Indexed Annuity Crediting Methods

There are four basic crediting methods that insurance companies use with indexed annuities. Most products will offer at least two, if not all four, of these methods. In all these examples, I will assume that the S&P 500 is the stock index that is used as the measuring stick of the return. In reality, there are a multitude of different indexes that are used. I'll cover that later in the chapter. While there are many different indexes you can choose from, almost half of all the money put into indexed annuities have returns based on the S&P 500.

INTEREST CREDITING METHOD #1: ANNUAL POINT-TO-POINT WITH A CAP

With the annual point-to-point with a cap crediting method, the insurance company looks at the value of the underlying index on each policy anniversary, then calculates the percent increase or decrease in the index. If the index increased in value, then a cap is applied, thereby limiting the return. If the index declined in value, then no interest is paid during that year. Visually, this method would appear as follows:

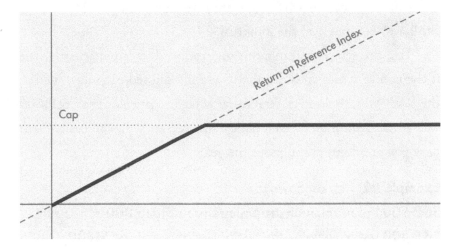

As the selected index increases in price, you get a return equal to the percentage increase right up to the cap. Once the cap is reached, you receive no additional interest, no matter how high the index goes.

Let's look at two simple examples—one where the market goes up and another where it goes down.

Example #1: Market upturn
S&P 500 index value on the policy issue date: 3,000
S&P 500 index value on the first policy anniversary: 3,300

On the policy issue date, the insurance company quotes you a cap of 4 percent. This is the most you can earn during the year, no matter how well the index performs.

In this example, the index goes up exactly 10 percent ((3,300 - 3,000) / 3,000). Since the cap is 4 percent, you will earn 4 percent. Had the index gone up just 2 percent to 3060, then you would earn the full 2 percent change in the index because the percentage change was less than the cap. This is a good time to point out that the index return does not include dividends. Only the absolute change in the price of the index is used to calculate any interest that is due. This is yet another reason why index annuities will not provide returns similar to equities over the long run.

You can see how simple this method is. This is particularly true if the contract uses an index that is readily quoted each day, such as the S&P 500. As long as you know what the price of the S&P 500 was at the beginning of each policy anniversary, you can easily track how you are doing throughout the year.

Example #2: Market downturn
S&P 500 index value on the policy issue date: 3,000
S&P 500 index value on the first policy anniversary: 2,800

On the policy issue date, the insurance company quotes you a cap of 4 percent.

Because the index dropped in value, you would not be credited any interest during your first policy year. Certainly no one likes to see no growth in their investment for a full year. And in reality, if the market goes down two or more years in a row, you could see no growth in successive years. Historically, the stock market goes up about three out of every four years, so two or more years in a row of 0 percent should be rare, but it certainly could occur. However, if that happens, it's likely most of your other investments have declined in value—probably significantly. Getting 0 percent might not seem so bad in such a situation.

INTEREST RATE CREDITING METHOD #2: ANNUAL POINT-TO-POINT WITH A PARTICIPATION RATE

This method works exactly like the first method, but rather than applying a cap, the insurance company gives you a percent of the change in the index. Visually, this method would be as follows:

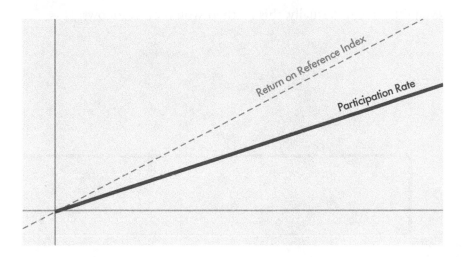

You can see how your return continues to increase as the price of the index increases; however, you only receive a specific percentage of the price change.

Let's look at the above example again, but rather than applying a 4 percent cap, we will assume a 30 percent participation rate. In the upmarket example, the insurance company would once again calculate the change in the index as 10 percent. It then applies the 30 percent participation rate to arrive at 3 percent to be credited to your account for the year. In the down year, you would, of course, still not incur a loss. You just won't earn any interest.

INTEREST RATE CREDITING METHOD #3: ANNUAL POINT-TO-POINT WITH A TRIGGER RATE

In my view, this is the simplest of all the crediting methods. Rather than quote you either a cap or a participation rate, the insurance company gives you a flat rate they will credit to your account as long as the index you choose does not go down in value during the year. As an example, if the trigger rate is 3 percent, then you will earn 3 percent whether the index is up 0 percent, 5 percent, 15 percent or even 40 percent. Visually, this method would be as follows:

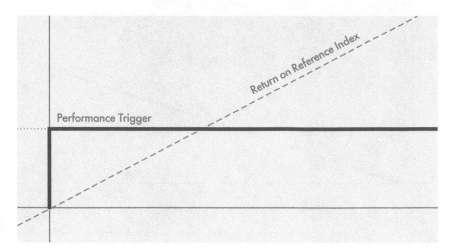

You can see that as long as the price of the index does not fall, you receive the full performance trigger rate. No matter how much the index goes up in price, as long as it is not negative, you get the same positive return.

And just like the other two methods, you will earn no interest in the years where the index declines in value. This trigger rate will always be less than cap rates that are offered at the time because the insurance company must credit that rate, even if the index is unchanged.

INTEREST RATE CREDITING METHOD #4: MONTHLY SUM

If an advisor is recommending an index annuity that can earn returns of 10 percent or more, he or she is probably referring to a monthly sum strategy. Typically, this strategy adds up all the monthly changes in the index, subject to a cap of no more than 2 percent per month. Therefore, if the stock market goes up for twelve months in a row, you could actually earn up to 24 percent for an entire year. But stop and think for a second. How often does the stock market go up for twelve straight months? For example, in 2021, a year where the S&P 500 went up 26.61 percent, the price of the index dropped during three of the twelve months.

This method works just like the annual point-to-point (method #1 above), but with one very notable exception: the cap is only applied on the upside, not the downside. Rather than look at the index value at year's end, the insurance company captures the value each month. However, rather than average the values, it sums the changes from one month to the next. Anytime the index is positive from month to month, a cap is applied (typically 1.5–3 percent) in order to smooth out the increases. However, typically no such cap is applied to any down months. This can actually lead to a negative return, even if the market goes up. Again, an example will probably help. For this example, I will assume a monthly cap of two percent on the S&P 500 index is applied on a policy issued on February 1.

February 1: 1,000

March 1: 1,020 for a change of +2 percent

April 1: 1,010 for a change of -0.98 percent

May 1: 1,040 for a change of +2.97 percent, therefore, the 2 percent cap is applied

June 1: 990 for a change of -4.81 percent

July 1: 1,050 for a change of +6.06 percent, therefore, the 2 percent cap is applied

August 1: 1,035 for a change of -1.42 percent

September 1: 1,025 for a change of -0.967 percent

October 1: 1,050 for a change of +2.44 percent, therefore, the 2 percent cap is applied

November 1: 1,060 for a change of +0.952 percent

December 1: 1,090 for a change of +2.83 percent, therefore the 2 percent cap is applied

January 1: 1,120 for a change of +2.75 percent, therefore the 2 percent cap is applied

February 1: 1,140 for a change of +1.78 percent

The insurance company would then add all these monthly changes—including the negative ones. This would result in a return of 6.555 percent on an index that increased 14 percent over the year. Of all the crediting methods, this will be by far the most volatile and is likely to have the least correlation to the actual market returns. In years when the market moves up and down throughout the year, the return is likely to be close to 0 percent or even negative (which would result in no interest credited during the year). On the other hand, if you have a year when the market goes steadily up, this will easily be the best performing method. In fact this occurred three times in the last fifteen years—in 2006, 2013, and 2021, the market went up virtually every month. In such years, this method will provide impressive returns, but it's certainly not a situation you should expect.

Comparing the Four Strategies

Each of these four strategies will perform the best in different market environments. Let's look at a few different scenarios and see which strategies should perform the best.

1. <u>The market consistently goes up.</u> Here the monthly sum will likely perform the best because it will capture gains in most months of the year and will have minimal impact from the few negative months. The second-best option would likely be the participation rate. If the market goes steadily up, it's likely to have a good year overall; therefore, you would benefit from

getting a percentage of the entire change for the year. If you choose the cap option, you will likely earn the full cap. And since the index did not drop, the performance trigger would pay you the full trigger rate.

2. <u>The market fluctuates during the year but finishes higher.</u> In this situation, the cap rate or the participation rate method will likely provide the best return. If at the end of the year, the market is up 12 percent or more, the edge will likely go to the participation rate. If the price increases 5–10 percent, then you will likely do best with the cap rate. If there is a lot of volatility, it is possible that the monthly sum rate could return close to 0 percent—especially if the down months drop 3 percent or more.

3. <u>The market is up 4 percent or less.</u> First, I should note that this rarely occurs. When the market goes up, it typically goes up more than 10 percent. Positive years of 0–4 percent are few and far between. But, when this does occur, the performance trigger will likely provide the best return because you will get the full-performance trigger rate and you will likely only get part of the cap rate.

4. <u>The market goes down.</u> In this scenario, which you should expect to occur on average one of every four years, it probably won't matter which method you choose. They are all likely to pay you no interest for that particular year. If at the end, the market drops only a little, it is possible that the monthly sum will provide a slight positive return. It will all depend on whether the positive months that are subject to the monthly cap will exceed the negative months.

Zero Is Your Hero

A key feature of an indexed annuity is the fact that the index price that determines your amount of interest is reset at the end of each crediting period (usually one year). Therefore, if the index drops in value during a specific year, you don't have to wait for it to recover back to its original price before you begin earning interest again. Essentially, a year of zero interest actually becomes your hero. A simple example can demonstrate the power of this feature.

Let's look at a hypothetical return on an index annuity tied to an index that stands at 1,000 on the day we fund the annuity.

The table below shows how the combination of locking in gains as you go, never getting a negative return in any selected index period, and the earning interest in any market-up year—despite the previous year's performance—can provide you a consistent and steady return.

How the Annual Reset Feature Works

	START	END		5% CAP	ACCT. VALUE
YEAR 1	1000	1200	+20% Increase	5% Growth	$105,000
	Locked Gains				
	START	END		5% CAP	ACCT. VALUE
YEAR 2	1200	900	-27% Loss	0% Growth	$105,000
	No Loss				
	START	END		5% CAP	ACCT. VALUE
YEAR 3	900	990	+10% Increase	5% Growth	$110,250
	No Recovery Needed				

Despite the fact that the index at the end of year three is below the value on the day the annuity was purchased ($990 versus $1,000), the annuity would have credited interest in two of the three years. If the index is up during your selected time period, you will earn interest.

If it's down, you will not go backward. You will simply earn 0 percent. You don't have to wait for the index price to recover before you are eligible to earn interest in a subsequent period.

Other Index Options

All the above examples assumes that the S&P 500 is the index that is used to calculate any earned interest. Due to its familiarity, as well as its proxy for the stock market as a whole, the S&P 500 is by far the most commonly used index. However, in reality, every indexed annuity will offer multiple different indexes—each designed to represent a different subset of the market. For example, if you want to tie your returns to a stock index that more favors technology stocks, you might look for an indexed annuity that offers returns tied to the Invesco QQQ index. If you want returns tied to foreign stocks, you might look for an indexed annuity that offers the MSCI World Index or the FTSE 100 index. Does it matter? In the long run, probably not. Certainly, there will be time periods where

EVERY INDEXED ANNUITY WILL OFFER MULTIPLE DIFFERENT INDEXES— EACH DESIGNED TO REPRESENT A DIFFERENT SUBSET OF THE MARKET.

certain indexes will outperform, but unless you are really good at predicting how stocks will move, you are just as likely to choose a particular index at a time which it will underperform as well as a time it will over perform. And if a particular index has historically outperformed other indexes, you are going to find that the insurance company will offer lower cap or participation rates on that index, thereby negating any expected long-term advantage.

VOLATILITY CONTROL INDEXES

Most indexed annuities will also offer unique indexes that were designed specifically for indexed annuities. Most of these are what the industry calls "volatility control" indexes. They are designed with one primary goal in mind: to smooth out returns in both up and down markets. I'm going to oversimplify this a bit, but essentially, these indexes are a blend of stocks, bonds, and cash. They contain automatic triggers that move the weighting between these three asset classes. When stocks get volatile, the index moves money from stocks to either bonds or cash. When stocks get less volatile, they will move money back to stocks. The goal is to avoid years of negative returns. To accomplish this, the index will also give up significant upside. It's simply not possible to earn 15 percent or more in a year when a significant portion of the index is sitting in bonds or cash. Despite this, there are two reasons that these indexes should be considered:

1. While the design of these indexes greatly limits the upside, it also greatly reduces the chances of getting a negative return in a given year. Even a 1–2 percent return in years when you would have otherwise earned 0 percent can make a big difference over time.

2. Due to the lack of volatility of the index, the insurance company can afford to give you much better rates. For example, if the participation rate on the S&P 500 is 40 percent, it might be 100 percent or more on these indexes. Therefore, it is still possible to earn 5–10 percent or more even if the index doesn't go up that much.

CONSIDERATIONS BEFORE BUYING AN INDEXED ANNUITY

While the concept of an indexed annuity is pretty straightforward, the number of options and variations that are available on most indexed annuities can significantly add to the complexity of the product. Here are the main things to consider:

1. <u>There is a cost to get out early</u>. Like most annuities, indexed annuities will have an early withdrawal fee known as a surrender charge. Typically, this fee will last for 5–10 years; therefore, you should be prepared to hold the annuity for at least that long. There is an additional 10 percent tax on any withdrawals prior to the age of fifty-nine-and-a-half.

2. <u>Indexed annuities are not a safe way (or better way) to invest in the stock market.</u> Purchasing an indexed annuity is not a substitute for investing in stocks. That's particularly true at today's interest rates. Indexed annuities are a potential substitute for bank CDs, money market accounts, and highly rated bonds. Their goal is to give you the most return possible without the possibility of losing money. Obviously, when safety of principal is the primary goal, your potential upside is always going to be limited.

3. <u>Make sure you understand the index or indexes on which your earnings are based.</u> Certain indexes, as well as certain crediting strategies will perform better in certain market environments than others. But that also means there will be market environments where they underperform versus other designs. Choose an index that you are familiar with and can easily track online.

4. <u>Indexed annuities will occasionally credit 0 percent.</u> Historically, the stock market goes down one in every four years. That means if you own an indexed annuity for ten years, you should expect to receive no interest in two or three of those years. If you are not OK with that, an indexed annuity is not for you.

5. <u>Your interest and principal are only as secure as the issuing insurance company.</u> Indexed annuities are backed solely by the assets of the insurance company. While strict regulations exist on how the insurance company can invest your money, indexed annuities are not FDIC insured.

SHOULD I CONSIDER AN INDEXED ANNUITY AT ALL?

If you have a portion of your money that you don't want to put at risk and you don't expect to need the money for at least five years, then the short and simple answer is yes. In this environment of historically low rates, if your goal is to protect your principal and earn more than what you can get from your local bank or from US Treasury bonds, your choices are limited. By simply being OK with not knowing how much you will get from year to year, indexed annuities can potentially pay you a bit more in the long run.

BY SIMPLY BEING OK WITH NOT KNOWING HOW MUCH YOU WILL GET FROM YEAR TO YEAR, INDEXED ANNUITIES CAN POTENTIALLY PAY YOU A BIT MORE IN THE LONG RUN.

VARIABLE ANNUITIES

What Are They, and Why Would I Want an Annuity That Is "Variable"?

Your first thoughts might be, Why would I want an annuity that is variable? I thought annuities were all about certainty and protection. How could anything variable be appropriate for me? The reality is that if you see the value of mutual funds and/or ETFs, you will likely also see the value of variable annuities. You see, at the end of the day, variable annuities are really just the insurance industry's version of a family of mutual funds. However, rather than buying a bunch of different mutual funds in order to get exposure to different asset classes (e.g., growth funds, bond funds, international funds), you can get that same exposure with a single variable annuity. That's because each variable annuity has a bunch of mutual fund options. Some variable annuities offer more than one hundred choices. These mutual funds within a variable annuity are called subaccounts. The insurance company simply places multiple mutual fund options within a single annuity contract. Think of it like a 401(k) plan that hopefully is available to you at work. Within a single 401(k) plan, you have the choice of many different investment options. You can invest in just one or any combination of the various options. Due to tax law restrictions, these variable annuity subaccounts have to be mutual funds that cannot be purchased outside of a variable annuity. In other words, you won't find your favorite Vanguard, Fidelity, or American Funds mutual fund within a variable annuity. However, what you will find is a fund managed by those same money managers with the exact same objectives and most of the same holdings. Essentially, the mutual fund companies set up a clone of their retail mutual fund that you may already own in order to make it available through a variable annuity as well.

At this point you might be asking, "If it's really just a family of mutual funds within a single annuity contract, why is it called a variable annuity?" While this would be a very logical question, this is really another one of those situations where the industry didn't stop to think about a more appropriate name. Like any mutual fund, the return each year will depend upon the actual performance of the securities owned within that fund. In other words, the return will be variable each year, hence the term. By now you are probably understanding why I sometimes shake my head at how the annuity industry decides to name and describe its products and product features.

Why Would I Buy a Variable Annuity Rather Than a Mutual Fund or Exchange Traded Fund?

TAX DEFERRAL

Because the mutual fund options are all within an annuity wrapper, you don't pay any taxes until you take money out of the annuity. In other words, the insurance company will not send you a 1099 showing any reportable income until you make a withdrawal. You can leave your earnings in the contract for as long as you want. If you still own the contract when you die, your beneficiary will be required to pay the taxes at their tax bracket when they receive the money. Mutual funds, on the other hand, must distribute capital gains each year; therefore, you will likely have taxes due even if you made no withdrawals. In fact, if you suffered from poor timing as to when you bought the fund, it's even possible for you to have to pay capital gains even if the value of your investment has dropped since you bought it. This was, in fact, the experience of many mutual fund holders in 2022. Despite recording significant negative returns for the year, most mutual funds distributed capital gains to their shareholders. Exchange traded funds, or ETFs for short, however, are another matter. They are taxed like individual stocks. You will pay capital gains (or losses) only when you liquidate the ETF.

The tax treatment of a variable annuity becomes even more beneficial if you plan to use the annuity as a means to increase or decrease your exposure to stocks over time. For example, let's say the market has done really well for a couple of years so you decide you should rebalance your portfolio in order to reduce your exposure to stocks. In fact, that would have been a really insightful decision toward the end of 2021. If you own mutual funds, ETFs, or even individual stocks, the sale of any of these assets will trigger capital gains taxes. In fact, it's not uncommon for investors to elect to not reallocate in order to avoid such taxes. I experienced such reluctance just prior to the internet tech crash in 2000. Shortly after

IF YOU OWN MUTUAL FUNDS, ETFS, OR EVEN INDIVIDUAL STOCKS, THE SALE OF ANY OF THESE ASSETS WILL TRIGGER CAPITAL GAINS TAXES.

my daughter's birth in 1995, I put $10,000 into two tech stocks to start funding her college education—$5,000 in Microsoft and $5,000 in Sun Microsystems. Amazingly, by early 2000, these two stocks were worth a combined $100,000. Common sense told me that such growth could not be sustained and that I should at least diversity the holdings to help preserve her college fund. However, any sale of either stock would create capital gains taxable to me, so I held tight. By the middle of 2002, the two stocks were once again worth just $10,000.

Had I funded this college plan by buying a tech based subaccount in a variable annuity, I could have sold some or all that position and moved it to a more conservative investment within the same variable annuity contract. Perhaps I would have elected not to make such a change because I believed the market was going to keep going up. I'll never know. But what I do know is that a big factor in my decision not to sell was the tax consequences of the investment vehicle I chose.

Here's the trade-off: When annuities of all kinds are eventually taxed, they are taxed as ordinary income. Mutual funds and ETFs, like most other investments, are taxed as short- or long-term capital gains. While the capital gains rate changes over time, it's almost always lower than the ordinary income tax rate. In addition, both mutual funds and ETFs get a stepped-up cost basis at death. Therefore, any unreported gains you would have when you die would be completely cancelled before the asset passes to your heir. Given these different tax implications, an important part of any decision as to whether to buy a variable annuity over a mutual fund or ETF is how long you anticipate holding the asset and what your expected tax bracket is when you plan to take the money out. A good general rule of thumb is that you should expect to own the variable annuity for ten years or longer for it to be a consideration. The longer you hold it, the greater the advantage of deferring taxes. In order to justify a holding period of much less than ten years, you had better be pretty certain you are going to be in a lower tax bracket when you take the money out.

GUARANTEE OF PRINCIPAL (OR MORE) AT DEATH

Most variable annuities include a guarantee of your investment upon death. In other words, if you invest $100,000 and then have the misfortune of dying when the value of your annuity has dropped in value—perhaps because an unexpected pandemic decimates the market—the insurance company is required to pay your beneficiaries the full $100,000 you invested. Typically, the cost of this guarantee is built into the annual cost of the annuity. However, an increasing number of variable annuities offer it as an option at a separate cost of 0.15–0.3 percent per year, and some variable annuities don't offer it as an option at all.

There has been considerable debate over the years whether this benefit is worth the cost. After all, over time the market goes up, so if you own the contract long enough, it should be worth more than you invested. In my mind, it's like any other insurance—you don't need it until you do. While it's true that the vast majority of policyholders will never need this guarantee, the fact of the matter is that the insurance industry paid out hundreds of millions of dollars in extra death benefits for years after the prolonged bear markets of 2000–02 and 2007–09. There's a few rules of thumb here too. First, the older you are, the more valuable the guarantee. The cost of this guarantee does not change based on the owner's age. Every variable annuity with a guaranteed death benefit charges a set percentage each year, regardless of the age of the owner. Therefore someone seventy or older is more likely to benefit from the guarantee than a fifty-year-old. In addition, this could be a good reason for an older investor to move money from mutual funds to a variable annuity. Consider a seventy-five-year-old who has owned mutual funds for the last five to ten years and does not anticipate needing most of those holdings during their lifetime. In all likelihood that investor would have seen considerable growth over the years. By moving some or all that money to a variable annuity, he or she would effectively lock in the current value upon death. Of course, making this reallocation would require the liquidation of the mutual funds (or ETFs or stocks), which in turn would trigger a taxable event; therefore, such a transaction should first be reviewed by his or her tax advisor.

In response to the criticism that guaranteeing the invested amount upon death might not be the most valuable guarantee, some insurance companies offer an option of enhanced death benefits at an extra cost. Essentially, the insurance company guarantees to pay the beneficiary the invested amount, plus some level of growth. These optional benefits each come at an extra cost. These designs typically come in three flavors.

Highest Anniversary Value Death Benefit

This option pays the beneficiary the greater of the initial investment or the highest value on any policy anniversary date. This has the effect of moving the death benefit up as the contract value increases. Then, if the contract value subsequently falls, the beneficiary is still entitled to the higher value. To consider how valuable this benefit can be, let's go back to the example of my daughter's college account. Had I put the original $10,000 into a variable annuity with a highest policy anniversary death benefit, the death benefit would have increased each year as it grew toward the $100,000 it ultimately reached. It would have remained there even if it fell all the way back down to $10,000. Of course, I would have had to die before she left for college in order to collect on the death benefit, but think of the peace of mind I would have had knowing that most of her college costs were taken care of if something unexpectantly happened to me. And what if something did happen to me? How valuable would that death benefit have been?

You should expect to pay an extra annual fee of about 0.25–0.5 percent per year for this benefit.

A Death Benefit That Increases by a Given Percentage per Year

This option increases the death benefit by a specified percentage per year—typically about 5 to 6 percent. This allows you to assure the client that the beneficiary will receive a minimum predetermined amount, provided there were no withdrawals and the contract is still in the accumulation phase (has not been turned into a stream of lifetime income).

You should expect to pay an extra annual fee of about 0.75–1 percent per year for this benefit.

Combination of Both Options

Can't decide between the highest policy anniversary death benefit and one that increases by a specified percentage? Consider one that combines the two. With this option, the beneficiary receives the greater of the highest policy anniversary value or the original premium growing at the specified amount.

Because this is a combination of the first two optional death benefits, it is going to be the most expensive. Expect to pay about 1–1.5 percent per year for this benefit.

ALL THESE OPTIONS WILL INCREASE THE DEATH BENEFIT ONLY UP TO A SPECIFIED AGE—USUALLY EIGHTY OR EIGHTY-FIVE.

It's important to note that all these options will increase the death benefit only up to a specified age—usually eighty or eighty-five. Once the owner reaches that age, the death benefit value is locked into place and will not increase. The reason for this is simple. An individual in their eighties has a much shorter life expectancy and therefore has a much greater chance of dying when the account value has dropped. By limiting the age, the insurance company reduces this risk.

What Should I Expect to Pay?

When you buy any annuity—including a variable annuity—the insurance company incurs the following costs:

- A commission is paid to the advisor that sold the annuity to you. For variable annuities, this commission is typically 4–7 percent of what you invested.
- The sales team employed by the insurance company to get your advisor to recommend their particular annuity over another company's variable annuity is going to receive a commission as well. Typically, this will be about 1 percent of what you invested.
- The insurance company has to process your application and issue you a physical policy. The cost of this administrative process is about 0.25–0.5 percent of what you invested.

If we total these three items, we get to a total cost to sell and issue your variable annuity between 5.25 and 8.5 percent. None of this cost is deducted from the amount you invest. The insurance company will front the cost and issue you a policy for 100 percent of what you invested. To recover this cost, the insurance company will assess what they call an annual mortality and expense and administration cost. Within the documents you will receive, this will likely be called and M&E&A fee, or sometimes just an M&E fee. You can expect this fee to be 1–1.4 percent of your account balance each and every year. This allows the insurance company to recoup, over time, the 5.25–8.5 percent in costs it incurred when it issued the policy. Each carrier will also incur about 0.3 percent in annual costs to administer your policy each year. Therefore, the annual fee you are assessed has to cover this ongoing cost as well. This fee also typically covers the fee of any built-in return of premium death benefit discussed previously.

In addition to the M&E&A fee, you will also pay an annual money management fee on each of the subaccounts in which you invest your money. This annual fee might be as low as 0.25 percent for a money market subaccount and as high as 1.5 percent on an international subaccount, or one that invests in more complex investment types such as gold or oil and gas. On average, you should expect to pay 0.8–1.2 percent per year. Most of this money goes to the firm that is managing the subaccount such as Fidelity, Vanguard, or American Funds. But some of this money is kept by the insurance company to cover the cost of keeping track of how much of each subaccount each policyholder owns, as well as sending you annual statements and other required regulatory mailings (e.g., that annual prospectus you will likely throw straight into the recycling bin).

Of course, any insurance company that gets into the annuity business is only going to do so if it expects to earn a profit. Let's just average out some of these numbers and add up the math.

- One-time cost to sell and issue the contract: 7 percent, plus

Paid for by assessing:

- Annual M&E&A fee: 1.2 percent
- Insurance company's share of money management fee: 0.5 percent

Subtract:

• Ongoing administration cost: 0.3 percent

You can see that it takes the insurance company about four to five years to break even. After that, profits begin to roll in at a pretty healthy pace—provided you keep the policy. If you cash in the policy after the five- to ten-year surrender charge, you become a marginally profitable client to them at best.

Variable Annuities That Don't Pay a Commission

While the vast majority of the variable annuities sold today pay a commission to the advisor that recommends the annuity, commission-free annuities do exist. In fact, each year they become a larger percentage of total sales. In the industry, they are referred to as advisory variable annuities.

Advisory variable annuities will differ from commissionable variable annuities in two ways. First, they will have a much lower M&E&A fee—typically 0.3 percent. Some only charge a flat monthly fee of $30–$50 and don't charge an M&E&A fee at all. When no commission is paid, there is much less upfront cost to recover; therefore, it's not necessary to charge such a large M&E&A fee.

COMMISSION-FREE ANNUITIES DO EXIST.

Secondly, advisory variable annuities will not have an early withdrawal or surrender charge. As I mentioned in the chapter on why people hate annuities, commissionable annuities have a surrender charge for the first three to ten years of the policy in order to allow the insurance company to recover all the costs it incurred to issue the policy, should you not stay in the policy long enough for the company to recover the costs through the annual fees generated by the policy. However, for the same reasons as the lower M&E&A fee, if there is no commission paid, then the company is not going to lose much, if any, money on you should you get out of the policy in the first few years.

Now, before you start concluding that the lower fees and lack of surrender charges must make an advisory annuity a much better deal, remember that there is no such thing as a free lunch. If an advisor is recommending an advisory annuity, then that advisor is going to place that annuity into an advisory account and charge you a fee each year to manage the money in that advisory account—including your annuity. A typical advisory fee is 1 percent per year. Rather than pay the insurance company via an annual policy fee, you will essentially pay the advisor directly.

None of This Sounds Too Complex

Variable annuities are often referred to by critics and regulators as a complex investment structure. Yet, I just took a few pages to describe how they work. If they are so complex, why isn't this chapter longer? At its core, variable annuities are really quite simple. You have a bunch of mutual funds wrapped into one contract. You can invest in any one or any combination of these funds. You can also move money between the funds every day if you want (although you will probably only be allowed to make twenty-five changes per year without an extra cost). You don't pay any taxes until you take money out, and then you pay ordinary income taxes on the gains. What makes variable annuities complex is the multitude of other options. These include:

1. Various death benefit options to protect your investment for your beneficiary.

2. Various income benefits to pay you an income for life—these benefits come in enough flavors that I've elected to give this topic its own chapter later in the book.

3. A multitude of annuitization options, should you decide to receive your lifetime income in a more traditional manner.

Not only must the insurance company explain these three things in full within both the contract you will receive as well as the prospectus, but it must also explain the following:

1. All fees and costs and how they are assessed.

2. The differences between the three parties that must be on every annuity (owner, annuitant, and beneficiary) and how they can relate to each other and can be changed.

3. A complete description of every subaccount, along with its individual fees and performance history.

Before long you have yourself a forty-page contract and a one-hundred-plus-page prospectus. The sheer size of these documents will lead almost anyone to conclude that a variable annuity is complex. In a way, it's a catch-22 for the industry. The very belief that the product is complex leads regulators to require additional disclosure within the application process as well as the product brochures and prospectus. But these additional disclosures lead to longer applications, contracts, brochures, and prospectuses, which in turn only confirms the belief that the product is complex.

Closing Thoughts

If each of the following sentences is true for you, you should consider a variable annuity. If even one of them doesn't resonate with you, you're probably better off just sticking with either mutual funds or ETFs.

1. You intend to set aside money for at least ten years and plan to make minimal, if any, withdrawals prior to the age of sixty.
2. You want to minimize the income taxes you pay each year on your investment.
3. You want to invest in stocks but like the idea of reallocating your investment without worrying about taxes.
4. You want to either protect the future income the investment will generate or protect what you plan to leave to your heirs.

STRUCTURED ANNUITIES

I would suggest that you save this chapter until you have some quiet time and can properly focus. You might even want to grab a cup of coffee (or a stiff drink) before you start reading. Structured annuities are by far the most complex of all the annuity variations. But because it can provide returns tied to the stock market without much of the potential downside, it is also the fastest-growing product segment. It doesn't help that the industry can't agree on a name for these types of products. I refer to them as structured annuities because they are the annuity version of structured notes—a type of bond that pays interest based on a stock index such as the S&P 500. However, they are also referred to as registered index-linked annuities (RILA), buffered annuities, and variable indexed annuities. Sadly, none of these names provide much insight into what this product does and how it works. But then, if they did, there would be less of a need for this book.

STRUCTURED ANNUITIES ARE BY FAR THE MOST COMPLEX OF ALL THE ANNUITY VARIATIONS.

In many ways, a structured annuity is similar to an indexed annuity. They both provide returns linked to a stock index while still offering some downside protection. The biggest difference is that an indexed annuity is designed to give you 100 percent downside protection. The worst you can do in any given policy year is 0 percent. Because an indexed annuity cannot go down in value from year to year, it's going to give you very limited upside. As I said in that chapter, it's an alternative to CDs, not stocks. A structured annuity, by comparison, gives you only partial downside protection. In fact, you determine how much protection you want. In exchange for accepting only partial protection, you get more upside—perhaps significantly more. The less downside protection you accept, the more potential return.

Does a Structured Annuity Make Sense for Me?

If you can answer "yes" to each of the next three questions, then I would suggest you continue reading this chapter. If, on the other hand, your answer is "no" to all these questions, then you can put down that cup of coffee and move on to the next chapter in the book.

1. Do you want to earn more than 5–6 percent per year, *on average*?
2. Are you OK with seeing your account value drop some, but not a lot, over a specified period of time?
3. Would you like to invest more money in the stock market but are worried that the market will fall significantly shortly after you invest?

If you answered "yes" to these questions, then a structured annuity could be a good alternative for you. By design, the goal of this type of annuity is to give you most of any market increases while limiting your downside. Note, however, that it only limits your downside. It does not eliminate it. However, since the market goes up over the long run, if you own a structured annuity for at least ten years, there is very little chance this product will not provide you with a positive return. Even a holding period as short as five years puts the odds heavily in your favor.

The Choices You Have to Make When Buying a Structured Annuity

Every structured annuity requires the policyholder to make four choices:

1. Choose the index on which your return will be based. The S&P 500 is the most common choice, but like fixed indexed annuities, every product will offer multiple indexes to choose from.

2. Choose the duration of the interest crediting segment. Over what length of time do you want the insurance company to observe the selected index before crediting interest to your account? Typically, the contract will offer choices of one, three, or six years.

3. Choose the amount of downside protection you want.

4. Choose the crediting method. Do you want to get 100 percent of the return of the index up to a limit (or cap), or do you want to get a specified percentage of the index return?

You might have noticed that these choices are very similar to the choices you must make if you buy an indexed annuity. In fact, three of them are exactly the same. The real difference between an indexed annuity and a structured annuity rests with the third choice above—how much downside protection you want. Given that this is the big difference between the two products, let's take a look at how this downside protection works.

How Much Downside Protection?

Typically, structured annuities will offer three methods of limiting downside exposure.

BUFFER AGAINST LOSS

Structured annuities typically come with several "buffer" choices ranging from 10 percent to 30percent. This buffer percentage represents the maximum amount of downside protection against a drop in the selected index. For example, if you choose a 10 percent buffer against the S&P 500, then you are fully protected against any losses up to 10 percent. If the index dropped by 5 percent over the period you chose, then you would not see any loss because it's less than your 10 percent buffer. Of course, you would earn no interest either since the index declined in value. If, on the other hand, your selected index dropped 15 percent over the time period you chose, then your account value would drop in value by 5 percent—the amount over your 10 percent buffer. Not surprisingly, the larger the buffer, the lower the upside potential.

FLOOR STRATEGY

This method uses tactics opposing the buffer method. With a "floor strategy" (sometimes called a "guard") option, you are exposed to the percentage loss up to the floor amount but are protected against any loss after the floor percentage. For example, if you choose a 10 percent "floor" then the maximum amount of loss you can occur during any period you select is 10 percent. If your selected index goes down 2 percent, you will lose 2 percent. If it goes down 5 percent, you will lose

5 percent. And, if it goes down 10 percent, you will lose 10 percent. However, that is the most you can lose over your selected time period. If the market crashes and goes down 20 percent, 30 percent, or more, your account will only fall by 10 percent. The insurance company must absorb any losses above that.

FIXED PERCENTAGE OF ANY INDEX DECLINE

One company offers a design that protects you against exactly half of any drop in the index you select. For example, if the index drops 10 percent, then you incur a 5 percent loss. If it drops 25 percent, then you incur a 12.5 percent loss. This downside protection amount is always fixed. What changes is the potential upside. Typically, this upside is between 70–80 percent. If it were 75 percent, then you would be entitled to exactly 75 percent of the increase of the index but be subjected to only 50 percent of the downside. Because the market typically goes up three out of four twelve-month periods, and big up years typically lead to more change than big down years, this formula can work out very well in the long run. For you blackjack players out there, it's similar to doubling down on a hand.

FOR YOU BLACKJACK PLAYERS OUT THERE, IT'S SIMILAR TO DOUBLING DOWN ON A HAND.

You choose to double down when the first two cards show that the odds are in your favor. You might still lose on any one particular hand, but over the long run, doubling down is a winning strategy. Since the fixed percentage strategy gives you 70–80 percent of the upside but only 50 percent of the downside, over the long run, this strategy should reward you with roughly 85 percent of the total market return with significantly less downside risk. Why roughly 85 percent even if it entitles you to only 70–80 percent of the upside? Because, historically, stocks have more big up years than big down years.

Deciding between the Three Options

When deciding between these three options, you need to consider two things. First, do you want to know the maximum amount of loss you can incur over a one-, three-, or six-year period? If so, then the floor strategy is the only one for you. The floor strategy limits any losses to a known maximum. With the other two strategies, while your loss is reduced, it is not limited and therefore not known. If you have a 10 percent buffer and the index drops 50 percent (which is highly unlikely, but possible), then you will incur a loss of 40 percent. Similarly, in such a scenario, the fixed percentage option would give you a loss of 25 percent.

Limit Any Potential Losses by Choosing a Longer Term

Remember, structured annuities typically offer terms of one, three, or six years. These terms represent the length of time that must pass

THE REALITY IS THAT THE LONGER THE TERM YOU SELECT, THE LOWER THE CHANCE THAT YOU WILL INCUR A LOSS.

before the insurance company calculates and credits your return. While it's always nice to see interest added to your account each year, the reality is that the longer the term you select, the lower the chance that you will incur a loss. The market is far more likely to be down in value twelve months from now than thirty-six months from now. And there is even a lower probability that it will be down six years from now.

What Should I Realistically Expect from a Structured Annuity?

Just like choosing between today's multitude of Oreo cookies (I prefer the Oreo Mint Thins myself), all the available choices make the decision process that much harder. Therefore, this is definitely a product where you want to get the help of a financial professional. To give you a sense of the trade-offs between protection and upside, let's take a look at the rates that were available on various structured annuities as of October 1, 2022.

ONE-YEAR TERM ON THE S&P 500

Let's assume that you either want to get interest credited to your account each year, and/or you want the flexibility to frequently change your investment options. If either is true, then you would likely want to choose a one-year term. Within the October 2022 market, you would have been offered the following one-year options on the S&P 500 index:

- 10 percent buffer with a maximum return (cap) of 20 percent
- 20 percent buffer with a maximum return (cap) of 12.5 percent
- 10 percent guard with a maximum return (cap) of 14.25 percent

Right away you can see the trade-off between potential upside and downside protection. Given these three options, the most you could earn over the next twelve months is 20 percent. Remember though, that doesn't mean you will get 20 percent. This is simply the most you could potentially earn. To get the full 20 percent, the S&P 500 must increase in value (without dividends) at least 20 percent during the year. If it only returns 8 percent, you would get 8 percent. On the other hand, if it returns 30 percent, you will still get 20 percent. To get the potential to earn 20 percent, you have to be willing to accept any loss above and beyond your 10 percent buffer. If the market falls less than 10 percent, you will earn no interest at all. If, on the other hand, it drops 15 percent, then you will lose 5 percent for the year.

If you don't get enough peace of mind from being protected against the first 10 percent drop in the market over the next year, you can choose the 20 percent buffer instead. However, now your upside is capped at 12.5 percent. As you add more protection, your potential upside drops even further. If you want to make sure you can lose at most just 10 percent (the floor strategy), then the most you will earn during the year is 14.25 percent.

HOW DO YOU DECIDE?

In order to choose between these options, we need to understand the odds of each event occurring. More specifically, we need the answers to the following questions:

- How often does the S&P 500 drop in value more than 10 percent over a twelve-month period? How often does it drop more than 20 percent?
- When the S&P 500 dropped more than 10 percent or 20 percent, how far beyond those buffers has it gone? Or, put another way, how much could I possibly lose based on historical market performances?
- If I choose the 10 percent guard, how often would I expect to lose money over a given year?
- What is the expected return of each of these strategies?

Fortunately, technology now exists to help answer these questions. By accessing this technology, we can test how each of these three options would have performed over every one-year period since 1953. The tables below summarize the results for each of the options.

S&P 500 ONE-YEAR PERIODS 1/2/1953–9/28/2022			
	10% BUFFER/ 20% CAP	20% BUFFER/ 12.5% CAP	10% FLOOR/ 14.25% CAP
PERFORMANCE			
BEST	20%	12.5%	14.25%
AVERAGE	8.7%	7.05%	6.18%
WORST	-38.82%	-28.82%	-10%
FREQUENCY			
POSITIVE	73.22%	73.22%	73.22%
ZERO	14.21%	22.78%	0.02%
NEGATIVE	12.57%	4.0%	26.76%

INTERPRETING THE ABOVE CHART

The Best Return

This number is simply the best return you can get in any one year. Since all three options have a cap, the best return is equal to that cap. If we look at only this criteria, we would take the 10 percent buffer with the 20 percent cap in order to capture the highest possible return. But remember, the more the upside potential, the greater the potential downside. Therefore, we need more information to make the best choice.

The Average Return

This is the return if we average the returns that would have been experienced in every one-year period back to 1953, assuming the cap rates listed above never changed from year to year and the stock market's performance is similar to how it has performed historically. In reality, the cap rates will change over time, but our goal in this example is simply to give you some indication of what to expect over time. Once again, due to the 8.7 percent average return, it appears as though the 10% percent buffer with the 20% percent cap is the superior option.

The Worst

This is the single worst one-year return over every one-year period after the buffer or floor is applied. All the sudden, the 20 percent cap with the 10 percent buffer doesn't look so good. Had you employed this strategy during the financial crises of 2007–09, you would have had a one-year period where the index was down 48.82 percent, leaving you with a loss of 38.82 percent after the buffer. And while the 20 percent buffer would have helped a bit, it would have only protected another 10 percent, thereby leaving you with a loss of 28.82 percent. Under these extreme conditions, the floor option shines. Since it protects you from any loss beyond the floor percent, you would have only experienced a loss of 10 percent.

Positive

This number gives you the percentage of times you would have experienced a positive return in a given year. If you remember, I have previously said that the market goes up on average about three out of every four years. This number proves that point. If we look at every one-year period since 1953, the S&P 500 increased in value 73.22 percent of the time. This means no matter which of these three options you select, you should expect to receive a positive return of 73.22 percent.

Zero

This number represents the percentage of time you would have historically received no interest in a year. You will note that for the 10 percent floor option, this occurs only in the years where the S&P 500 ends a year exactly where it started. Historically, that has happened only 0.02 percent of the time—or pretty much never. For the 10 percent buffer/20 percent cap, it has historically occurred during 14.21 percent of the total one-year periods. In other words, the index was down for the year, but by no more than 10 percent. When we move up to the 20 percent buffer, we are also protected from any time where the S&P 500 falls in value between 10–20 percent, thereby our probability of zero return increases to 22.78 percent.

Negative

This number represents the percentage of times you should expect to get a negative return of any amount. In other words, the buffer or floor didn't fully protect you. You will notice that the floor strategy has the highest percentage of negative results at 26.76 percent (or that one in four again). This is because the floor doesn't protect you against a loss; it limits your loss to no more than 10 percent. Therefore, any time the S&P 500 falls in value, you will have a loss of between 0 and 10 percent. We see the least loss occurrences with the 20 percent buffer. Historically, the S&P 500 drops more than 20 percent over a one-year period only 4.07 percent of the time, or about one in every twenty-five years.

Investment Tidbit: The Importance of Timing

This example illustrates how important timing can be in investing. Consider the difference in results for the person who selected a three-year structured annuity period on March 1, 2006, as compared to the person who selected the exact same option just three years later. One would be down over 30 percent, while the other would have earned almost 75 percent. The only thing that changed was the dates. Did the person that bought in 2006 make a worse decision than the person who bought in 2009? No. One just had better timing. The lesson here is to focus on the long-term and stay the course. Don't worry about daily, or even yearly, changes in values. When it comes to structured annuities, this also makes the case for choosing a longer investment option. Let the market work for you over time.

THREE- AND SIX-YEAR TERM ON THE S&P 500

Structured annuities also give you the option of selecting either a three- or six-year strategy. The downside to this is that you have to wait three or six years before you get interest credited to your account. But by selecting a longer term, you are also automatically getting more downside protection. Simply put, the odds of the market going down 20 percent over a six-year period are significantly less than the odds of it going down 20 percent over the next twelve months.

If we once again look at rates available on structured annuities in October of 2022, we find the following rates.

- 10 percent buffer with a maximum return (cap) of 500 percent
- 15 percent buffer with a maximum return (cap) of 400 percent
- 25 percent buffer with a maximum return (cap) of 125 percent

Using the same technology we used to look at the one-year strategies, we can summarize the results of the six-year strategies as well. Keep in mind that these performance numbers are over a six-year period, not annual. Therefore, the average return of 61.44 percent on the 10 percent buffer option represents the average interest credited after the six-year period, not each year.

S&P 500 ONE-YEAR PERIODS 1/2/1958–9/28/2022			
	10% BUFFER/ 500% CAP	15% BUFFER/ 400% CAP	25% BUFFER/ 125% CAP
PERFORMANCE			
BEST	243.11%	243.11%	125%
AVERAGE	61.44%	61.6%	57.67%
WORST	-29.89%	-24.89%	-14.89%
FREQUENCY			
POSITIVE	87.21%	87.21%	87.21%
ZERO	8.23%	10.85%	12.09%
NEGATIVE	4.55%	1.94%	0.69%

This example shows us how a bit of information provided by technology can help us make what I would call a clear choice. On the surface it would look like the chance to earn 500 percent over six years with a 10 percent buffer is much better than an opportunity to earn "only" 125 percent over that same six years due to accepting a much larger 25 percent buffer. After all, how often does the market go down more than 10 percent over a six-year stretch? Surely, that would be enough protection, so we might as well take the greater upside.

However, the reality is that the market doesn't go up 500 percent over six years. In fact, we see the that during single best six-year period it went up "only" 243.11 percent. Therefore, while 500 percent sounds great, it's just not going to happen. Nor is 400 percent. And that 10 percent buffer over six years? We would still have almost a one in twenty-five chance of not providing enough protection. In my view, the only logical choice given the pricing above is to take the extra protection of a 25 percent buffer, thereby reducing the chances of experiencing a loss down to less than 1 percent. Yes, our average return drops from 61.44 percent to 57.67 percent, but isn't that trade-off worth it in order to reduce the chances of a loss from about one in twenty-five to one in one hundred? You might draw a different conclusion. You might not worry about a one in twenty-five chance of losing money and want the opportunity to earn over 200 percent. Nothing wrong with that. But this also reflects the tremendous flexibility offered by structured annuities. You can decide the appropriate risk versus reward trade-off that works best for you. And of course, as prices change, your conclusions might change with them. For example, if the cap rate on the 25 percent buffer option falls from 125 percent to 75 percent, the expected average return might fall enough to have you consider an option with a higher cap and a lower buffer.

WHAT IF I HAVE TO GET OUT OF MY CONTRACT BEFORE THE END OF MY SELECTED TERM?

First, I will say that if there is a good chance that you will need the money before the end of the rate guarantee period you select, then you shouldn't buy the annuity. But I realize that unexpected situations occur. All structured annuities have a formula built in that will give you a pro-rata portion of any gains that occur up until the date you liquidate the annuity. These formulas will vary from company to company and can be extraordinarily complex. The bottom line is that while you will capture some of your earnings, you will likely leave a good portion behind. The closer you are to the end of the interest rate period when you cash out, the less you will leave on the table. But my advice here is simple. If you are not confident that you can hold the structured annuity until the end of the term you select, don't buy it in the first place.

Unique Indexes

In an attempt to differentiate their product versus their competitor's, some advisors will offer a proprietary index in addition to the well-known indexes such as the S&P 500 or the Russell 2000. Just like the unique indexes found in fixed indexed annuities, almost all these unique indexes are designed to smooth out the ups and downs of the market. They will have a specific formula that will move money back and forth from stocks to bonds and/or cash. The goal is that as the market gets more volatile and begins to fall, the index will automatically move money out of stocks and into bonds and/or stocks. Conversely, as stocks start to rise, the formula will move money out of cash and/or bonds and into stocks. At least, that's the theory.

The goal here is to reduce the chances that you will have a negative return during the interest-crediting period you selected. It's hard to argue with that goal. After all, one of the main reasons people buy a structured annuity is to get downside protection. If the index itself can provide that protection, that must be a good thing, right? Well, maybe or maybe not. Most of these indexes target a certain level of stock market volatility—typically 5–10 percent. The index will only be fully invested in stocks if the market volatility is at that level or lower. However, the average stock market volatility is closer to 15 percent. That means that the times you will be fully invested in stocks will be few and far between, which in turn means your upside with most of these indexes is greatly reduced. But if you think about it, that makes perfect sense. If the index is designed to reduce your potential upside, it must also therefore reduce your potential upside. You simply can't have one without the other.

The design of these indexes also allows the insurance company to quote higher caps and participation rates. For example, if a one-year term on the S&P 500 has a cap of 20 percent, the cap on the volatility proprietary index might be 100 percent or more. How is this possible? It's very simple. If the odds are very small (or pretty much nonexistent) that the index will provide such a return, it's really easy for the insurance company to offer something that is not likely to happen. While the quoted caps and participation rates are important, the likelihood of the index achieving those rates is equally, if not more, important.

IT'S REALLY EASY FOR THE INSURANCE COMPANY TO OFFER SOMETHING THAT IS NOT LIKELY TO HAPPEN.

It's also important to note that the insurance company stands to benefit from you selecting an index that is less likely to go down in value. Remember, they have to cover any losses beyond the downside protection you selected. If you chose a 10 percent floor strategy because you want to know you can't lose more than 10 percent, then the insurance company has to cover any loss more than that. If the index is designed to reduce the chances that it will fall more than 10 percent during the selected period, then the chances of them having to cover any losses goes down as well.

None of this is to say that you shouldn't select a unique volatility controlled index. You just need to understand that it comes with a trade-off. Make sure you understand the following:

1. How is the index put together? What is the expected percentage of stocks, bonds, and cash within the index?
2. How will the allocation between stocks, bonds, and cash change over time?
3. What type of return can I expect versus the S&P 500 in an average market environment?
4. What is the actual track record of this index?

The last point is particularly important because many of these indexes have been designed within the last several years and therefore have a very limited track record. Because of that, most of them will have a hypothetical "back-tested" track record. To calculate this back-tested return, the company that designed the index uses market data to replicate what the index would have done had it existed earlier. However, there is a major flaw to such a methodology. No two markets are ever the same. Just take interest rates. Not long ago, interest rates were near historic lows. You simply can't compare today's markets with today's rates to ten years ago and assume similar results.

Make sure your advisor has access to the technology I've referred to in this chapter. The flexibility and choices that come with every structured annuity allow you and your advisor to customize a product to meet your specific needs. But to do this accurately, the advisor must understand the trade-offs between the various options. Without the data I've used in the examples in this chapter, an advisor is mostly guessing. Yes, he or she will intuitively know that a six-year option has less downside exposure than a one-year option. In addition, he or she will know that a larger buffer will provide extra protection than a smaller buffer. But unless he or she can quantify those trade-offs, it's difficult, at best, to choose the right option.

Who Should Consider a Structured Annuity?

While a couple of structured annuities have now come to market with a living benefit designed to provide income in retirement, this product type is still bought mostly as a way to build retirement assets by giving you a means to participate in the market while still giving you some downside protection. Therefore, while similar to all other types of annuities where policyholders have the option to annuitize structured annuities, they are not typically purchased as a source of retirement income. They are mostly about tax-deferred growth. This makes structured annuities an appropriate option for individuals who want to be in the market but will quickly get nervous if headlines start screaming, "Stocks plunge." Structured annuities are also a good option for someone who has built considerable retirement assets and wants to take some risk off the table. Rather than selling stocks and moving to bonds as a means to add protection, this individual may elect to stay exposed to equities but add the extra protection provided by the protection features offered by structured annuities.

SINGLE PREMIUM IMMEDIATE ANNUITIES AND DEFERRED INCOME ANNUITIES

Single premium immediate annuities, otherwise known as SPIAs, are the purest form of an annuity. When you buy a SPIA, you give the insurance company a lump sum of money (the single premium) and they in turn provide you an income for a) a specific number of years; b) over your life; c) over the life of you and someone else; or d) some combination of the first three options. I cover these options in detail in the following chapter on annuitization. To qualify as a SPIA, the first income payment must be made to you within twelve months of you buying the annuity. Insurance companies also offer deferred income annuities (DIA). When you buy a DIA, your first income payment will be made to you more than a year after you purchase it. In most cases, it will be years later. For example, you might buy a DIA at age sixty with the plan to begin receiving income when you retire at age sixty-five or seventy. You select the age at which the payments begin.

Although annuities were originally designed to provide an income for life, few annuities are purchased for solely this reason. In fact, SPIAs and DIAs make up only about 3 percent of total annuity sales. While a significant number of annuities will eventually be used to generate income, they are typically first bought for the accumulation benefits they offer, such as tax-deferred growth or protection of principal. SPIAs and DIAs are purchased solely for the income they provide—either immediately or many years later.

The first thing you need to know about buying either a SPIA or DIA is that they are both irrevocable transactions. Once you make the commitment to buy the SPIA, you can't later change your mind and ask for your money back. But that's not all bad. In fact, you actually benefit in two ways from this lack of liquidity. First, since the insurance company knows that it has just entered into a lifetime contract with you, it can invest your money for a longer term, thereby allowing them to maximize what they can earn on the money you invested. This allows the insurance company to pay you a greater amount of income. The second benefit is really more emotional rather than financial. Both SPIAs and DIAs give you the peace of mind that you will get a check in the mail for the agreed-upon time period no matter what happens in the financial markets or your own financial situation. No matter how great the temptation to cash out, it's simply not an option under the terms of the contract. These annuities may therefore protect you from making what could turn out to be a poor long-term financial decision during a time of emotional or financial stress. A few companies do offer some SPIAs and DIAs that have limited liquidity, but these will always come at the expense of income. To offer any level of liquidity, the insurance company will need to guarantee less income per $1 invested.

> **SPIAS AND DIAS ARE PURCHASED SOLELY FOR THE INCOME THEY PROVIDE—EITHER IMMEDIATELY OR MANY YEARS LATER.**

The Concept of Mortality Credits

If you choose to get an income for life, the insurance company will primarily consider two things when calculating how much they will pay you: how much interest they can earn on the money you give them and how long they expect you to live. The more they can earn, they more they will pay you. On the flip side, the longer you are expected to live, the less you will get each year. As an example, females on average live several years longer than males; therefore, they will get less annual income per $1 of premium than a male. Over the years, some have argued that this is discriminatory against women. The reasoning goes that it simply isn't "fair" that they get less income than men. However, in reality, they aren't expected to get less. Yes, they will get less per year, but since they will live longer, they will get the payment for a longer time period. Over their expected life, men and women will get the same return on the premium they paid.

But what if you die sooner than expected? Doesn't that mean you lose and the insurance company wins? In a sense, you do lose because you would have received less income relative to the premium you paid than the person that did not die early. But, since you are dead, you probably don't care. But it's not the insurance company that wins, it's the person that lives beyond their life expectancy that is the winner. The insurance company pays everyone based on how long they are expected to live on average. They know that for every person that dies early, there will be a person that lives longer than expected. The insurance company uses the money they didn't have to pay to the person that died early to pay the person that lived too long. In the insurance world, this transfer of payments is referred to as "mortality credits." If person A dies at age seventy rather than eighty, then the insurance company essentially takes the savings from person A and credits that money to person B, who lives until ninety rather than eighty.

Here's the big takeaway from this entire concept: the people who will benefit most from annuitizing an existing annuity or buying a SPIA will be those that live beyond their life expectancy. Therefore, if your parents or grandparents have a history of living a long life, odds are that you will as well. That in turn means that you have a good chance of being the recipient of mortality credits rather than the one that is the source of mortality credits.

HOW SPIAS AND DIAS FIT INTO A FINANCIAL PLAN

Step one of every financial plan is to determine how much income you will need in retirement. This income amount is typically broken into two parts—essential expenses, such as food, utilities, healthcare, and mortgage payments, and nonessential expenses, such as travel and entertainment. Step two is to make an estimate of how much guaranteed income you will have in retirement. This is typically the sum of your expected social security benefits and any pension you might have. For most people, their essential expenses will exceed their level of guaranteed income. If that is not the case for you, congratulations. You can skip the rest of this chapter. For the rest of you, the final step is to determine how you will close that gap. One solution is to generate enough income from your investment portfolio to cover that gap. This income typically comes in the form of interest payments on bonds or bond funds you own and dividends from any stocks or mutual funds. If that is not sufficient to cover the gap, then you have to either reduce your essential expenses or liquidate some of your investment portfolio each year.

Annuities are another option. If I know the size of the income gap, then when I retire, I can put enough money into a SPIA to generate an income equal to the income gap. As an alternative, I can buy a DIA to provide the necessary income starting at the age I expect to retire. While both the SPIA and DIA will obviously take a chunk out of your investment portfolio—especially if you have a large gap— You can also invest the remaining funds in your portfolio solely for growth, without worrying about generating income. You don't have to worry about the income fluctuating as a result of a bond maturing or a dividend getting cut. SPIAs and DIAs not only give you peace of mind, but they also greatly simplify any retirement income plan.

USE A DEFERRED INCOME ANNUITY TO LAYER IN AN ADDITIONAL LEVEL OF INCOME

As mentioned above, DIAs are often bought to create an income stream that coincides with the age at which you expect to retire. For example, a fifty-five-year-old might buy one to begin income at age sixty-five. However, a second use is to create additional income years after you retire. The cost of your essential expenses will rise as you progress through retirement. Healthcare costs typically escalate because the cost of healthcare in general increases faster than most other expenses, as well as the fact that as you get older, you will likely need more care. Think about how comforting it would be to know that a new income stream (i.e., personal pension) is scheduled to begin at age seventy-five, eighty, or eighty-five. As a planning tool, pre-retirees will sometimes buy a DIA between the ages of fifty-five and sixty-five with the income starting ten to thirty years later. Due to the power of compound interest, it can be surprisingly cheap to buy an income stream that doesn't start until years down the road. For example, a fifty-five-year-old husband and wife could buy an income of about $33,000 per year to begin at age eighty for only $100,000. Of course, the other reason this income can be funded with so little money is that once you both hit eighty, your combined life expectancy is much shorter. But what happens if you both die prior to reaching that age? Are you just out the money? In all probability, the answer is yes. But remember, the goal here is to ensure a certain standard of living even if you live well into your nineties. You need to think of the DIA as a type of insurance rather than an investment. If you die early, it just means you never needed the insurance. Plus, as I also mentioned earlier, once you're dead, you won't care. It is possible, however, to buy a DIA that will return your invested amount to your beneficiaries should you die early. However, once again, this will come with the cost of lower income per dollar invested.

BUYING MULTIPLE DIAS

One common strategy is to buy multiple DIAs, each with a different start date. Perhaps one kicks in at age seventy-five, another at age eighty, and a final one at age eighty-five. The first DIA would provide the bulk of the income and would therefore require the majority of the purchase amount. Since each subsequent DIA would only need to provide enough additional income to maintain the policyholder's standard of living and would start at a later age, it would need a relatively small amount to fund. For example, a sixty-year-old might put $100,000 into a DIA that begins paying $17,085 per year at age seventy-five. In addition, that same client might put just $15,000 into a DIA that would begin providing an annual income at age eighty. The additional $3,785 in income would serve to protect the original income stream from inflation.

CHANGING THE INCOME START DATE ON A DIA

Some DIAs allow the policyholder to move up the income start date. Of course, the amount of the monthly payout could potentially be adjusted down if you choose a policy with this option. In addition, if you choose to move up the income start date, the original amount of income you were quoted will be reduced to reflect the longer period of time the insurance company now has to pay out the income. Despite these two considerations, I recommend that you consider this feature. Even the most thoughtfully crafted retirement plan can be upset by an unexpected job loss or illness. Should you be one of the 20 percent of retirees who were forced to retire earlier than expected due to illness or job loss, you will be glad that you can start the income earlier than expected.

Considerations before Buying Either a SPIA or a DIA

FINANCIAL STABILITY OF THE INSURANCE COMPANY

Since you're funding a lifetime income stream, it is essential that you only consider buying a contract from a financially strong insurance company. This is especially true when you buy a DIA since you may be waiting years before the income starts. Since any insurance company can experience financial difficulties if it incorrectly prices a product and/or invests premiums into an asset class that performs significantly worse than expectations, it can be a challenge to know which companies are built to last for decades. However, there are a few key traits that can attest to the annuity provider's financial strength and ability to continue operating as a going concern. The provider should be relatively large, it should maintain a relatively high credit rating from more than one of the major rating agencies, and it should maintain a healthy amount of capital to protect itself from potential problems. Every insurance company must publish a risk-based capital (RBC) ratio. Simply put, this ratio represents the amount of capital it holds relative to the minimum allowed by regulatory guidelines. For example, a company with an RBC of 400 percent is holding four times the amount of capital the regulators require. When buying any annuity, look for an RBC of at least this level. Also, look for a company that has a sizeable life insurance block. Life insurance and DIAs (as well as SPIAs) present offsetting risks to the insurance company. If Americans start living longer because we cure catastrophic illnesses like cancer, the insurance companies will have to pay out more annuity income than they previously expected. However, this also means that they will be paying significantly lower life insurance claims since people won't be dying as quickly as expected.

ALWAYS GET A QUOTE BEFORE ANNUITIZING AN EXISTING ANNUITY

Every annuity gives you the option of exchanging the value of your annuity for an income payment. That's what makes it an annuity. However, the amount of income you can get for each $1 of value you have can vary considerably from company to company, and even from product to product issued by the same insurance company. If and when it comes time to start receiving income from your annuity, ask your insurance company how much you can get for each of the various options available in your contract. Then go get a quote from several companies that offer SPIAs. If you don't want to do this yourself, any financial advisor with a life insurance license can help you. It's very possible that you can get more income by moving your existing annuity to a SPIA from another company. After all, since this is an irrevocable decision, the goal is to get the most income you can.

NEVER OVERLOOK THE VALUE OF AN OLDER ANNUITY

Even if you don't follow financial markets very closely, you probably realize that even with the recent increases, interest rates are much lower today than they were ten to fifteen years ago. We see this when we're offered 0 percent financing for sixty months or see that our bank has credited little, if any, interest on our savings. But this also means that annuity contracts issued more than ten years ago likely offer more guaranteed income than any contract you can buy today. Remember, one of the two assumptions insurance companies make in determining how much income they can offer is what can they earn on your money until they pay it all back to you. Today, they are likely to assume they can only earn 5-6 percent. However, fifteen years ago, they would have assumed 7-8 percent. Go back twenty years or more, and they would have likely assumed returns much higher than that.

If you have a contract that is at least 15 years old, make it the first asset you use to create retirement income. It will likely pay you 10–20 percent or more income than any annuity you can buy today.

The Bottom Line

As comforting as it is to have a source of guaranteed income other than just social security, it's hard to decide to turn over a significant portion of your retirement savings to an insurance company in exchange for that guaranteed income. You've worked hard to accumulate those savings over the years. There is something very satisfying at getting a statement with a large balance on it. It can be shocking to get the first statement after buying an SPIA or DIA because that

THAT LIFETIME INCOME STREAM IS WORTH A LOT— BOTH FINANCIALLY AND EMOTIONALLY. statement will be lower by the amount you used to purchase the annuity. You'll likely feel as though you just gave something up. However, that lifetime income stream is worth a lot— both financially and emotionally. The average person will receive $1,657 per month in social security, assuming that person started receiving

social security at age sixty-five and lives until eighty-five, the value of that twenty-year income stream at the time it begins is approximately $300,000. That's a true financial benefit. As for the emotional benefit, you'll truly understand that when that first check arrives.

WHAT HAPPENS WHEN I ANNUITIZE MY POLICY?

While many annuities are purchased mostly for the ability to accumulate money without paying taxes until the interest is received, all annuities give you the option of "annuitizing" the policy. When you annuitize your policy, you give the value of your policy to the insurance company in exchange for an income payout. In fact, it is this very concept for which annuities were originally designed centuries ago. The ability to grow money on a tax-deferred basis didn't become a popular concept until about fifty years ago. These annuity payouts can be for a specific time period (e.g., ten years), for as long as you live, or for as long as you and your spouse live. Typically, the income payments are made to you each month, but you can get them quarterly, semiannually, or annually. It's all up to you.

It can be very hard to just turn over a significant portion of your retirement savings. Quite frankly, probably less than 10 percent of all annuity owners end up doing this. However, in my

> **WHEN YOU ANNUITIZE YOUR POLICY, YOU GIVE THE VALUE OF YOUR POLICY TO THE INSURANCE COMPANY IN EXCHANGE FOR AN INCOME PAYOUT.**

view, the primary goal of retirement planning is to sleep well at night no matter what is going on in the world—socially, politically, or financially. Knowing that you will receive an income every month even if you live to be 120 years old is a very good sleeping pill.

The ad below appeared in a 1966 issue of Life magazine. Given that my copy is a copy of a copy of a copy, thereby making the text difficult to read, I have transcribed the text.

"How We Retired in Fifteen Years with $300 a Month"

LIFE magazine ad, January 21, 1966

Look at us! We're retired and having the time of our lives … Let me tell you about it.

I started thinking about retiring in 1950. Nancy thought I was silly. It all seemed so far away. "And besides," she said, "It makes me feel old." It didn't seem silly to me though. We had just spent the afternoon with Nancy's aunt and uncle. Uncle Will had turned forty-five during the war, and by 1945 his working days were over.

Now life seemed to be standing still for them. They couldn't even take the short weekend trips their friends could afford. They couldn't visit their children as often as they liked. A pretty grim existence, I thought. But why? He'd had a great job. Then Nancy reminded me—they had never planned ahead. During her uncle's working years, his paycheck was spent almost as soon as it arrived. Fortunately, they had put some money away for a rainy day, but they hadn't planned ahead enough to make those retirement days sunny.

Not for me, I decided. When it's time for us to retire, I want to be able to do the things we always dreamed of doing instead of counting every penny. I showed Nancy an insurance company ad I saw in Life magazine a week or so before. It described their retirement income plan, telling how a man of forty could retire in fifteen years with a guaranteed income of $300 or more for life. Nancy agreed it was a great plan. The thought of retiring at fifty-five didn't make her feel old at all! So I filled in the coupon that day and sent it right off.

A few days later, the booklet describing the _____ insurance company plan arrived. I picked the right one for us and signed up right away. Three months ago, my first check arrived—right on time.

Last month we moved down here to Florida, and we love it. Nancy looks great with her tan, and she's thrilled at the thought of keeping it all year long! My tan suits me fine, but I'm really hooked on the fish. Whether I catch one a day or seven (or more), I'm having the time of my life, because we saved for a rainy day with ____ insurance company.

Send for a free booklet.

This story is typical. Assuming you start early enough, you can plan to have an income of $50 to $500 a month or more beginning at age fifty-five, sixty, sixty-five, or older. Send the coupon and receive by mail, without charge or obligation, a booklet that tells about _____ insurance company plans. Similar plans are available for women—and for Employee Pension Programs. Send for your free copy now. In fifteen years, you'll be glad you did.

I can't help but chuckle every time I read this ad. As if the corny references about retiring to Florida aren't enough, the thought of being happy about living the good life on $300 per month just boggles my mind. The ad shows the happy, smiling couple sitting in a small fishing boat, holding up a fish they just caught. I can't help but think, facetiously, that the couple in the ad is smiling because they successfully caught their dinner for the evening rather than because they are having the time of their lives. And retiring at fifty-five? Three hundred dollars might have been able to cover substantially more in monthly living expenses than it can today, but that amount would still have to sustain them for almost forty years of retirement based on today's expectations of longevity.

PEOPLE STILL WANT THE SAME THINGS OUT OF RETIREMENT NOW THAT THEY DID IN 1966.

As dated as it is, this ad still portrays both the good and bad aspects about getting an income by annuitizing your policy. It does indeed give you a monthly check for life, but it also must be large enough to outpace years of inflation.

The ad is remarkable for another reason: people still want the same things out of retirement now that they did in 1966. People still want the assurance of a steady retirement check that they cannot outlive. Change the retirement age to sixty-five rather than fifty-five and update the income amount by a factor of ten, and this ad could describe an important financial goal of many of today's baby boomers.

Annuity Options

A common criticism of immediate annuities is the belief, misguided in my opinion, that payouts stop as soon as you die. Potential investors seem to have this concern that the excitement of receiving their first check will induce a heart attack and cause them to drop dead, thereby allowing the insurance company to keep the balance of the investment. Such a statement would be true only if you purchased a life-only annuity, and that is an option almost no one chooses. In fact, a life-only annuity would make sense only if you have no heirs that need income upon your death (including your spouse) and the goal is to receive the largest possible income check with the least amount of money. Even under those circumstances, few would be willing to buy a life-only annuity for fear of "losing to the insurance company." With that in mind, I will describe the more popular and suitable immediate annuity options.

To understand how the various options affect the income payments, you need to understand two concepts. First, the greater the contingent guarantees, the lower the income payment. This is why the life-only annuity option always pays the most money. The insurance company is basing the payments on a single life with no other contingent guarantees. Second, the older the individual upon whom the income is based (the annuitant), the higher the payments. The reason for this should be obvious: the older you are, the lower your life expectancy; therefore, the shorter the length of time the insurance company expects to have to make payments.

1. Joint and survivor annuities pay an income based on two lives. Upon the death of the first individual, the payments will continue at either 100 percent of the original income or a smaller percentage, such as 67 percent (under the

assumption that one can live more cheaply than two). This is a common choice for spouses. The benefit of choosing a reduced-income percentage upon the first death is a higher initial income since the insurance company is on the hook for a lower payment upon the first death.

2. With cash refund annuities, should the individual(s) receiving the payments die before the total income payments equate to the initial amount invested, the insurance company will pay the beneficiary the difference in a lump sum. As an example, if you annuitize $100,000 in exchange for $7,000 per year and then die after ten years, you would have only received $70,000 in total annuity payments. The insurance company would therefore send a $30,000 check to the beneficiary you listed on the policy. This is a popular option because the policyholder knows that the insurance company cannot pay out less than the amount originally invested. This option overcomes the concern that the insurance company will "win" if the policyholder does not live to his or her life expectancy.

3. Installment refund annuities are very similar to cash refund, except the insurance company continues to pay the income payments to the beneficiary until the amount originally invested is paid out. Once that occurs, the income payments stop. Sticking with the example in the cash refund option, rather than paying out the additional $30,000 in a lump sum, the $7,000 annual payments would continue until the additional $30,000 is distributed, four or more years from now. The advantage to this option over the cash refund option is that you will get more income initially. This is possible

because the insurance company knows it can pay the extra $30,000 out over time rather than a lump sum.

4. Life and term-certain annuities pay income payments for the greater of the life of the annuitant or the length of the term-certain period, typically ten or twenty years. If you die prior to the term-certain period, payments will be made to the beneficiary until the term-certain period ends. For example, if you choose a life and twenty years term-certain, but you die after fifteen years, the payments will continue to your beneficiary for the remaining five years.

These various options can impact income amounts differently. Take a look below at the side-by-side comparisons of income that would be paid out to a sixty-five-year-old and a seventy-five-year-old, both of whom invested $100,000, in immediate annuities.

PAYOUT OPTION	AGE 65	AGE 75
Life Only: Male	$612 (67% tax free)	$819 (81% tax free)
Life & 10 Years: Male	$604 (66% tax free)	$766 (74% tax free)
Life & 20 Years: Male	$516 (66% tax free)	$578 (69% tax free)
Joint & Survivor 100%: Male & Female	$477 (70% tax free)	$591 (86% tax free)
Cash Refund: Male	$578 (63% tax free)	$727 (69% tax free)

All the above calculations assume a policy issued in Florida as of October 1, 2022.

You can see how the income drops as the guarantees go up. There is only a slight drop in income between the life-only and the life-and-ten-years-certain options for the sixty-five-year-old, because it is highly likely the owner will live to at least seventy-five. Therefore, the additional guarantee by the insurance company is not that costly.

However, once you go to life and twenty years certain, you see a significant drop in income. The life expectancy of a sixty-five-year-old male is less than twenty years; therefore, guaranteeing the income for twenty years has significant cost. The insurance company offsets this cost by paying less income.

You can also see the big increase in income for the seventy-five-year-old. This is obviously due to the shorter life expectancy. The older the policyholder is, the more the income is driven by the policyholder's life expectancy and the less it's driven by interest rates (more on that later). This makes immediate annuities a particularly attractive alternative to older individuals.

SHOULD I PAY EXTRA FOR A COST OF LIVING ANNUITY OPTION?

Any of the above annuity options can also be purchased with an increasing annual payment of a specified percentage, typically 3 percent. On the surface, this option seems to make complete sense, and it would significantly boost income for the couple in the Life magazine ad, who would not have to rely on just $300 per month for the rest of their lives—even if the dollar's buying power was stronger in the late 1960s than it is now. In my opinion, this option is simply not worth the cost. Obviously, if the insurance company promises to increase the income payment each year, it is going to give the policyholder less money initially. For example, if the sixty-five-year-old couple in the above example elected to take a cash refund option with a 3 percent annual increase, they would only receive $388 per month, rather than the $477 per month without the annual increase. With the income increasing 3 percent per year, it will be year seven before they reach the amount of income they would have had in the first year had they not chosen the annual increase. At that point, they would both be seventy-two years old. Rather than purchase a cost of living annuity (COLA) on the annuity, I would suggest that you utilize the rest of your portfolio to generate future income needs. For example, this particular couple would have to put 23 percent more into a 3 percent COLA annuity to get the same initial income as the annuity without the COLA. Rather than put the extra money in the annuity, I would suggest they use those funds to buy either a mutual fund or variable annuity. Then you can use that money to provide additional income in later years—either by making systematic withdrawals or using the money to buy additional annuities every five or ten years.

WHAT TYPE OF RETURN WILL I GET ON AN ANNUITIZED POLICY?

We've all been trained to think in terms of rates of return when comparing various investment and savings options. Which bank pays the most on a one-year CD, which bond will pay me the most interest, and which stock pays the highest dividends? Not surprisingly, therefore, it is not uncommon for someone to base their decision on whether they should annuitize an annuity on the rate of return they expect to receive. However, when it comes to annuities, the

THERE IS ONE VERY IMPORTANT THING I DON'T KNOW—HOW LONG YOU WILL LIVE.

answer to this question is far from clear. There is one very important thing I don't know—how long you will live. If you can tell me the day you will die, I can easily calculate the return the annuity will provide because I would know how much you annuitized, the amount and frequency of the payments you will receive, and the length of time you received those payments. Since no one knows your exact date of death, all I can estimate is your expected return should you live to your life expectancy. A good estimate of this expected return is always ten-year Treasury rates, plus 1 percent. As I write this in late 2022, ten-year Treasuries are about 4 percent. Therefore, if you annuitize an annuity and live exactly to your life expectancy, the insurance company would have paid you about 5 percent on your money.

While many conservative investors would likely be happy with such an expected return, many financial advisors are confident that they can do better by managing and generating income from your retirement portfolio. But as I previously stated, an income for life is about much more than a rate of return. It's also about peace of mind. It's about knowing that income check will arrive each month no matter how long you live or how the market performs. It's about not worrying. It's about that sleeping pill. Would you end up with more income and more money left over for your heirs if you don't buy an annuity? Probably. In fact, there is a high likelihood that you will. But will you always wonder if some unexpected event might occur that will make it necessary for you to cut back on your standard of living in order to avoid running out of money before you die? If so, is it worth giving up a few points in additional return not to have to worry about that?

HOW ANNUITY PAYMENTS ARE TAXED

Annuities not only allow you to grow your money tax deferred, but they also provide some tax advantages when you elect to receive your money through annuitization. As you receive the income, the payments will be partly a return of your original investment and partly interest. In this way, it's much like a mortgage payment. When you make a mortgage payment, part of your payment is principal to pay down the loan and part of it is interest. Annuitization works the same way. The insurance company uses your life expectancy to calculate an "exclusion ratio." This exclusion ratio represents the percentage of each payment that is a nontaxable return of your original investment. In the previous table, this exclusion ratio is shown as the percentage of each payment that is a tax-free return of your original investment. This exclusion ratio percentage does not change from payment to payment until you have received back all your original investment. At that point, your income becomes 100 percent taxable. The good news here is that this means you have lived beyond your life expectancy.

Example:

A fifty-five-year-old male buys a $100,000 annuity, which grows to $200,000 by age sixty-five.

The life expectancy of a sixty-five-year-old male is eighteen years, or age eighty-three.

The insurance company agrees to pay him $13,000 per year for as long as he lives.

The total expected payment is $234,000.

The exclusion ratio is the initial investment as a percentage of the total expected payments: $100,000/$234,000 = 42.7%

The 42.7 percent of $13,000 each year is nontaxable, equating to $5,555. The remaining $7,444 would be reported as interest income.

If the individual in the above example is still alive at age eighty-three, then all the payments become taxable. But what if he chose an income payment option that stops when he dies, and he doesn't live until age eighty-three? This would mean he didn't get back his entire

$100,000 original investment and reported too much income. If this occurs, his estate would be allowed a deduction on his final tax return for the excess interest previously reported.

Note #1: Exclusion ratios only apply to nonqualified annuities (those bought outside of retirement plans).

If the annuity is being held in a retirement plan such as an IRA or 403(b), then the tax rules of that particular plan apply. For example, all money held in a regular IRA is pretax and therefore, there is no investment to return tax-free. All annuity payments would therefore be fully taxable.

Note #2: Only income payments made via annuitization receive an exclusion ratio.

If you elect to receive your annuity income via a guaranteed living benefit that is added to the policy, you are actually making withdrawals from the annuity. You have not turned over your account value in exchange for annuity payments. Therefore, these payments will be considered 100 percent taxable income until you have received all the credited interest. Once you have received all the interest and then start to receive your original investment back, there is no reportable income. Using our example above, the sixty-five-year-old who has $100,000 in tax-deferred interest, the first $100,000 received via a guaranteed lifetime withdrawal benefit is taxable. Once that is depleted, payments are taxable only to the extent of any interest credited since your last withdrawal. These type of living benefits are covered in detail in a subsequent chapter.

WHO GETS THE TAX BILL?

This is a critical point: regardless of who receives the income payments, the policyowner pays any taxes due. In addition, if payments are made to someone other than the owner, the owner is deemed to have made a taxable gift to the recipient of those payments. These rules are clearly designed to keep people from using annuities as an estate-planning tool.

Keep things simple. Ensure that the owner and the annuitant are the same party, (always a good rule for annuities) and name as the beneficiary whoever they want to receive any additional payments when the owner/annuitant dies.

UNDERSTAND THE DIFFERENCE BETWEEN CASH FLOW AND RATES OF RETURN

Far too often people quote the annual cash flow created by an immediate annuity as the rate of return. I once found a Modern Business book series printed in 1944 on the shelves of a vacation house my family rented. One book in this series was simply titled Insurance. I was intrigued enough to give the book a quick read. I couldn't help but wonder how much the advice about insurance had changed in eighty years. The author laid out a scenario of a $1,000 annuity that pays $69.66 per year, and they state that the "apparent rate of return for the money invested is 6.966 per cent," thereby giving us evidence that immediate annuity returns have been commonly misquoted for decades. As I stated earlier, unless you know exactly when you will die, calculating the actual yield on the annuity is not possible. But the error in the book goes well beyond that. Remember, when you annuitize a policy, a portion of each payment is a return of your original investment plus interest. Therefore, in the example in the Insurance book, a significant portion of the $69.66 per year is a return of the original $1,000 investment. It is not all interest; therefore, it is factually incorrect to quote a "6.966 per cent" rate of return. What you are actually receiving is a cash flow of 6.966 percent that is partially interest and partially a return of your original investment. Sadly, it is not uncommon for the rates of return on an annuity to still be quoted this way.

Given the uncertainty of your date of death, the first question you need to ask yourself is, "Am I happy with the amount of money the insurance company is paying me in exchange for what I have to give them?" The second, and most important, question is, "Will I sleep better knowing that check will arrive even if I live to be 120 years old?"

WHY PEOPLE ARE TOLD NOT TO ANNUITIZE THEIR POLICIES

As I mentioned at the beginning of this chapter, despite the need and desire for an income for life, a very small percentage of annuities are ever actually annuitized. I believe this is the case for the following reasons:

1. Most financial advisors simply don't think it's necessary. While an increasing number of financial advisors position themselves as full-service financial planners, most of them still think of themselves as investment advisors rather than financial advisors. If I'm an investment advisor, then I'm telling you that I'm good at investing your money. And if I'm good at investing your money, I will have no problems growing your retirement portfolio as well as providing you the income you need in retirement. Why would I outsource the income piece to an insurance company if I can do it myself? In most cases, they will be right. If you've saved

enough, they will be able to generate sufficient income for as long as you live. But why worry about it at all? If that financial planning software says you have a 90 percent chance of success, do you really want to take the chance you will be one of the one in ten that will run out of money? I don't.

2. Annuitized policies are a terrible investment (the implied rate of return is too low). If you take the emotions out of the decision and solely look at your choices based on the expected rate of return, you will likely conclude that the expected return on an annuity payment is too low relative to other retirement income solutions. As I said repeatedly in this chapter, for many people, it's not about the rate of return. It's about getting a check they can't outlive. I'm guessing you have never bothered to think about the rate of return on either your social security payments or your pension, if you are lucky enough to have one. You likely just want to know how big the check is.

3. If you die, the insurance company keeps all your money, This is true only if you choose a life-only annuity. Almost no one does. And certainly no one has to. There are plenty of options that guarantee that you or your beneficiaries will receive at least the value you annuitized.

ESSENTIALLY, YOU ARE FUNDING YOUR OWN PENSION IN EXCHANGE FOR EXPERT ASSET MANAGEMENT.

4. I don't want to give up control of so much of my retirement savings to the insurance company. It is true that you essentially give up control of the money in exchange for a stream of income. Essentially, you are *funding* your own pension in exchange for expert asset management. Why is that such a bad idea? How

often does someone ever want to turn his or her pension or social security payments into cash? Keep in mind, also, that you are not the only one that is giving up control of this asset. Your financial advisor will be giving up control as well. Given that his or her business model is built on the concept of accumulating and managing assets, don't be surprised therefore if your financial advisor is not a fan of annuitizing your annuity.

5. Policies shouldn't be annuitized when interest rates are low. Although I now see frequent articles about the benefits of using annuities to set up an income for life, these articles often come with a recommendation to wait until interest rates move back up. Since interest rates help determine the amount of income an annuity will provide you, the basic premise behind the recommendation to wait is that it makes little sense to lock in a lifetime income stream at today's con-tinually low interest rates. However, such advice is typically based on a lack of understanding of how annuities are priced. You see, unlike CDs and bonds—both of which are priced based primarily on interest rates and length of maturity—a significant portion of the income you will receive from an annuity is based on your life expectancy. In fact, the older you are, the greater the impact of your life expectancy relative to the current level of interest rates. Therefore, as interest rates consistently fell over the most of the last three decades, on a relative basis, the amount of income paid on newly purchased immediate annuities has declined significantly less than other low-risk investments that are often used for retirement income.

Good Reasons for Not Annuitizing

The most obvious reason for not creating income from an annuity is that you just don't need it. If you've successfully saved for retirement and been able to accumulate a sum that is greater than what any financial model shows you will need, then other than to just gain some additional peace of mind, there is no reason to use an annuity. Apart from that basic premise, there are three other factors to consider.

YOU EXPECT TO NEED ACCESS TO YOUR MONEY

While some insurance companies allow you to cash out your annuitized policy, such an option is an exception, not the rule. And if that option is available, you can bet that the insurance company is going to cash you out for far less than your future annuity payments are worth. Therefore, any decision to annuitize

ANY DECISION TO ANNUITIZE A POLICY SHOULD BE VIEWED AS AN IRREVOCABLE DECISION.

a policy should be viewed as an irrevocable decision. If you expect to have a need, or even could have a need for the money required to buy the annuity, you should likely look for another way to create a retirement income.

YOU HAVE A SHORT LIFE EXPECTANCY

Insurance companies offer income on annuities based on interest rates and average life expectancy. Therefore, those who will benefit the most financially from annuitizing are those who live beyond their life expectancies. Every year that one lives beyond his or her life expectancy is one more year of payments that the insurance company did not expect to pay to you. But the opposite is true for anyone who doesn't live to their life expectancy. In addition, the shorter your life in retirement, the less likely you will run out of money even if you just take a certain percentage of your total assets each year. Of course, no one knows how long they will live, but if your parents and grandparents died relatively young and/or you are in poor health, you should think twice before using annuities for lifetime income.

AN IMPORTANT FINANCIAL GOAL IS TO LEAVE MONEY TO OTHERS

By using a significant percentage of your retirement assets to buy guaranteed income in the form of an annuity, you are likely going to end up with less money when you die. To put it simply, you now have less money set aside to grow. Unless you are willing to invest the remaining assets more aggressively than you would have without the additional guaranteed income, the simple fact that you have significantly reduced your pool of assets means that you are likely to have less available for your heirs and/or charities.

Creditor Protection: One Last Potential Benefit

In most states, annuitized policies are protected from creditors and are not eligible for seizure in bankruptcies. This obviously makes this an attractive option for professionals who are subject to liability lawsuits, such as doctors. If the thought of creating a guaranteed income that can't be touched even by creditors appeals to you, speak to your tax advisor about the annuity rules in your states.

GUARANTEED LIFETIME WITHDRAWAL BENEFITS

A Newer Way to Generate Income for Life

Annuities have always been one of the only ways to generate an income for life. However, while getting a guaranteed check each month for as long as you live is an attractive idea for most, few have proven to be willing to hand over a chunk of their retirement savings to an insurance company in order to make this happen. As a result, about twenty years ago, the insurance industry developed a new alternative called a guaranteed lifetime withdrawal benefit (GLWB). More generically, this benefit is referred to as a living benefit. Like a traditional form of annuitization, the insurance company guarantees you a set amount of income each year for as long as you live, or even over the joint lives of you and your spouse. But unlike a traditional annuity, you are not making an irrevocable decision by turning over a large amount of money to the insurance company. You maintain control over your account and can choose to stop the income payments if you want. In addition, if there's still money in your account when you die, the beneficiary can choose to take that remaining amount in a lump sum.

Living Benefits Are Really a Guaranteed Systematic Withdrawal

For the last several decades, many retirees have lived off of the 4 percent rule. Essentially, this rule says that if you limit annual withdrawals from your total retirement account to 4 percent of the current balance, you should have enough money to sustain this rate of withdrawal no matter how long you live. The key word here, however, is "should." Every financial-planning software can model this out and will tell you the probability of the 4 percent rule working for you, given assumptions of how much money you have and how long you expect to live. Most financial planners shoot for a probability of 85–90 percent. What this essentially says is that based on historical market performance, you have an 85–90 percent probability that you will be able to make that 4 percent withdrawal each year and never run out of money. While that certainly puts the odds heavily in your favor, it still leaves at least a one in ten chance that you will run of money before you die. The chances of running out of money only go up if you live longer than expected. If you don't want to take a chance that you will be one of the unlucky 10–15 percent, then you can simply reduce the withdrawal rate to 2–3 percent. However, for anyone that does not have a pension to combine with social security, such a low withdrawal rate requires a large sum of retirement assets. Let's look at the difference even a small reduction in your withdrawal rate can mean for the amount of money you must save in order to get the same amount of desired income.

Example:

Both Investor A and Investor B determine they need an extra $50,000 per year in retirement income. Investor A elects to take 4 percent of her savings each year. Investor B wants to have a higher level of certainty that she won't run out of money before she dies, so she decides to take out only 2.5 percent each year.

How much money does Investor A need to save? $1,250,000.

$1,250,000 x .04 = $50,000

What about Investor B? $2,000,000

$2,000,000 x .025 = $50,000

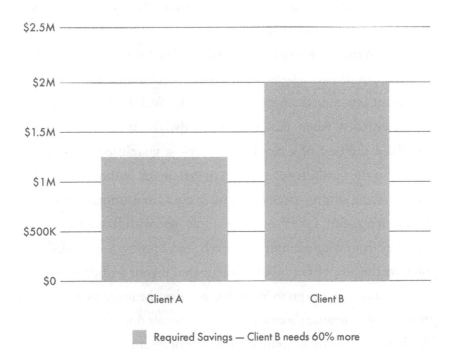

Required Savings — Client B needs 60% more

Accumulating $1.25 million is hard enough. Raising the goal to $2 million will be well out of reach for all but the wealthiest Americans.

The fact of the matter is that the 4 percent rule, even with today's interest rates, will likely not only allow you to sustain withdrawals for your lifetime, but is also likely to leave behind a considerable sum of money for your beneficiaries. The rule is designed to be overly conservative to protect against the possibility that you suffer from bad timing as to when you start the withdrawals. As I covered in the chapter on why the sequence of returns is important in retirement planning, a significant market decline shortly after your retirement date can put you in a hole so deep it can become almost impossible to dig out of it. Limiting withdrawals to just 4 percent is a means to help protect you from that situation. Such a low withdrawal percentage keeps you from creating an even bigger hole should the stock market start the digging for you. As an alternative, you can protect against poor timing by choosing to insure your retirement income. That's exactly what a GLWB does for you.

YOU CAN PROTECT AGAINST POOR TIMING BY CHOOSING TO INSURE YOUR RETIREMENT INCOME. THAT'S EXACTLY WHAT A GLWB DOES FOR YOU.

Essentially, when designing GLWBs, the insurance industry combined the best of a regular annuity—a guaranteed income for life—with the flexibility of a 4 percent systematic withdrawal. Rather than receiving annuity payments, you make a fixed annual withdrawal from your account. Like the 4 percent rule, you withdraw a set amount of money from your account value each year. However, with a GLWB, you have the peace of mind of knowing that if your withdrawals cause your account value to go to $0 before you die, the insurance company promises to continue those annual withdrawals out of its own funds. Think of it as buying insurance on your retirement income. If you are one of the unlucky ones who sees your account value depleted before you (or you and your spouse) die, then you essentially have a claim against the insurance company. This of course assumes you follow all the rules stipulated in the GLWB. More on that in a minute.

The Income Account: It's Not Money, but It Is Important

Of course, the mechanics behind a GLWB are more complicated than I described. Nothing in the annuity world is simple. GLWBs are certainly no exception. First and foremost, you have to pay extra to add GLWB to your annuity—typically about 1.5 percent per year. Think of it as the annual premium you pay for insuring your income. This fee is deducted directly from your account value each year. When you add a GLWB to your annuity, the insurance company establishes a second account that is associated with the policy. This second account is your income account. Unfortunately, this is yet another example of the industry not agreeing on terminology. Depending upon the company, this account can be referred to as the guaranteed withdrawal base, income base, or guaranteed withdrawal account. Because it's the account that establishes how much income you can get each year, I will refer to it as your income account.

A GLWB Adds a Second Account to Your Policy.

Regular Account Value: This is your actual money. How it will grow depends upon how you choose to invest the money. You can access it anytime you wish (early withdrawals will be subject to possible charges).

Income Account: This account is not actual money. It is used to calculate how much guaranteed income you can get for life—similar to how credit card points can be cashed in for travel and merchandise. It will grow each year at the rate specified by the insurance company when you buy the annuity. The more it grows, the more income you will get.

The most important thing you must understand about your income account is that it is not actual money. It is a value that is used to calculate how much income you can get at any point in time. The insurance company calculates this by multiplying the income account by a specified percentage. This percentage increases as you get older and you own the policy longer. For example, if your income account is 100,000, the insurance company might guarantee you an income equal to 5 percent of that account beginning at age sixty-five. However, if you take this money, it comes from your account value, not the income account. In reality, the income account is not an account at all. It is merely a number used to calculate how much income you can get. In that sense, it's similar to credit card reward points you might see on your credit card statement. You might have 300,000 points, but they are certainly not worth $300,000. Credit card points are merely a number that is used to calculate your reward. That's exactly how the income account works. Despite this, every annuity company insists on putting a dollar sign in front of the income account number you will see on your statement, thereby leading many annuity policyholders to believe that this balance is actual money. In this book, you will never see a dollar sign in front of any income account I use in an example. To do otherwise would be a mischaracterization of the value of the account.

HOW THE INCOME ACCOUNT IS CALCULATED

At the outset, the income account is always equal to the amount you put into the policy. Therefore, if you buy a $100,000 annuity and elect to add a GLWB to the policy, your initial income account will be 100,000. The insurance company will then guarantee to grow this account by a specified percentage each year until you begin taking income from your policy. This growth percentage rate is typically 5–7 percent per year. For GLWBs added to variable annuities, the insurance company will typically only pay this growth rate for ten to twelve years. If you still haven't started taking income from the annuity at that point, your income account will stop growing. For indexed annuities, the income account will usually grow for twenty years or longer. You always want to make sure you plan to begin taking the income no later than the time frame at which the income account stops growing. Therefore, if it only grows for ten years, you shouldn't purchase a living benefit more than ten years before you plan to start taking income.

How much money you can take out each year depends on two things:

1. The age you are when you start taking income—the older you are, the more you can take.
2. Whether you are taking income over your lifetime or over the lifetime of you and your spouse. You will get more if the payments are guaranteed only for your life and less if they are guaranteed for two lifetimes.

Let's look at a couple of examples:

Example #1: A sixty-five-year-old male buys a $100,000 annuity with a GLWB and starts to take income over his lifetime immediately.

The initial income account will be 100,000—the same value as the account value.

Is there any growth in the income account? No. Since the income is started right away, there is no time for the income account to grow. All future income will be based on this 100,000 number.

How much can I take each year? Typically, a GLWB will allow a sixty-five-year-old to take 5 percent of the value of the income account each year for life. That would therefore create a lifetime income of 5,000 (100,000 x .05). Should the policyholder elect to receive the income over two lives, then the allowable withdrawal will be lower—perhaps 4 percent or 4.5 percent rather than 5 percent. This lower percentage is designed to offset the additional risk the insurance company takes by guaranteeing the payments for two lives rather than one.

Remember, this money comes from the account value, as does the annual fee for the GLWB. Therefore, if the GLWB fee is 1.5 percent, or $1,500, and the withdrawal is 5 percent, or $5,000, then $6,500 is being taken out of your account value each year. That means that if the investment options you have chosen for your account value don't earn at least $6,500 each year, your account value will decline over time. Eventually, it will go to $0. You can begin to see the risk the insurance company is taking here. Let's assume that the stock market goes down during the first year and the account value falls 10 percent or $10,000. Due to the $5,000 income withdrawal plus the $1,500 fee, the account value is now worth only $84,500. Yet, the owner of the policy still has the right to take $5,000 the following year because, while the account might fall in value, the income account does not.

AS LONG AS THERE IS MONEY IN YOUR POLICY, YOU ARE JUST PAYING YOURSELF.

As long as the owner does not take more than the allowed $5,000, the income account will always be 100,000. Since you have insured your retirement income, the ups and downs of your account value will have no impact on that level of income.

WHY THE INSURANCE COMPANY GROWS THE INCOME BASE WHILE YOU WAIT TO TAKE INCOME

The simple reason here is that the older you are, the lower your life expectancy. Therefore, you should be rewarded for waiting to take the income by getting more income when you finally start to take it. But there is another reason as well. Remember, all income payments come out of your own account value first. The insurance company only has to pay your income out of its own pocket if you run out of money. As long as there is money in your policy, you are just paying yourself. Therefore, the insurance company wants to encourage you not to take the income for as long as possible. The longer the account value lasts, the lower the chances that they have to begin paying your income out of their money rather than yours. In addition, they have more years to collect the annual fee (your insurance premium) for providing the income guarantee.

Example #2: A sixty-five-year-old male buys a $100,000 annuity with a GLWB but waits until age seventy to begin taking income.

The initial income account will still be 100,000—the same value as the account value.

Is there any growth in the income account? Yes. Because no money is taken out of the annuity during the first five years, the income account grows each year. For this example, we will assume the growth is 5 percent each year. That's a pretty typical growth rate, but some contracts will grow the income account at a higher rate.

What will the income account equal after five years? 125,000. Most product designs today use a simple interest rate rather than a compounded interest rate. A simple interest rate will credit the exact same amount each year. In this example, 5 percent of 100,000 equals 5,000, so that is the amount that will be credited each year. A compounded rate of interest will credit the 5 percent on not only the initial 100,000 but the amount added to the account each year. Therefore, in year two, a compounded rate of 5 percent would mean you would get 5 percent on 105,000 rather than the initial 100,000. Everything grows faster—much faster—at a compounded rate rather than a simple rate.

How much can I take each year? Not only has the income base increased to 125,000, but because the owner of the annuity is seventy rather than sixty-five, the insurance company will allow him to take a greater percentage of the income account—probably 5.5 percent rather than 5 percent. This increased withdrawal rate reflects the fact that the owner is older and has a lower life expectancy.

125,000 x .055 = $6,875

By waiting 5 years, the owner will now get 37.5 percent more income.

The bottom line here is that the more you know about when you want to start taking income, the more effective GLWBs are as a retirement-income tool. If you are not sure when you will need to take income from the annuity—or whether you will need to do so or not—then you are increasing the chances that you are going to pay for insurance that you don't need.

The Concept of a Step-Up: Your Path to More Income

In the previous example, I illustrated a situation where the allowable income increases only because we waited to take the money. But what if the account value grows faster than the income account? Shouldn't you benefit from such a scenario? Yes, you should. And due to the concept of an income account "step-up," you will. If on any policy anniversary, your account value is greater than your income account, your income account will step up to the value of your actual account. Since your income account grows, so will your allowable income.

Let's go back to the second example, where the sixty-five-year-old purchaser elects not to take income until age seventy. On the first policy anniversary, we know the income account will grow from 100,000 to 105,000. But let's assume the account value earned 10 percent net of fees, thereby increasing from $100,000 to $110,000. On each policy anniversary, the insurance company compares the account value to the income account. If the account value is greater than the income account, your income account will be stepped up to the value of the account value. In this example, the income account would step up from 105,000 to 110,000. This obviously increases your income as well, because now you would be entitled to 5 percent of 110,000 rather than 5 percent of $105,000. In addition, the 5 percent growth on the income account is now applied to the new, higher value.

The following table shows how this concept might work for our fictional sixty-five-year-old who expects to take income at age seventy. I've assumed various returns, both positive and negative for the account value. You will see that on each policy anniversary, the income account is increased to the greater of the account value or the previous year's income account growing at 5 percent.

POLICY YEAR	INCOME ACCT. GROWTH @ 5%	ACCT. VALUE	NEW INCOME ACCT.	AVAILABLE INCOME (AGES 65–69: 5%) (AGE 70: 5.5%)
0 (Age 65)	100,000	$100,000	NA	$5,000
1 (Age 66)	105,000	$110,000	110,000	$5,500
2 (Age 67)	115,500	$112,500	115,500	$5,775
3 (Age 68)	121,000	$130,000	130,000	$6,500
4 (Age 69)	136,500	$132,000	136,500	$6,825
5 (Age 70)	143,000	$110,000	143,000	$7,865

HOW A "STEP-UP" INCREASES THE INCOME ACCOUNT VALUE

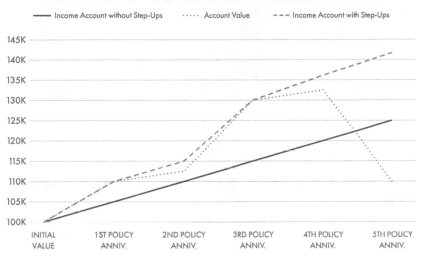

When the policy was originally purchased, we knew the income account would grow exactly 5,000 per year and therefore be equal to 125,000 at age seventy. This is represented by the solid line on the above graph. Think of this as the worst-case scenario. No matter what happens to the account value, this is the least amount the income account will ever be. And since we know the income account would be 125,000 and the policy allows you to take 5.5 percent of that income account at age seventy, we know that we will have a guaranteed income for life equal to $6,875 (5.5 percent of 125,000). The contract in this example had two step-ups—one in the first year and one in the third year. This is represented by the dashed line. You can see how in both years one and three, it increases at a faster rate than it otherwise would have. The growth in the account value pushes it higher. By age seventy, our income account is 143,000, which allows for annual income of $7,865. That's $990, or 14.4 percent higher than we expected when we bought the policy five years earlier. Finally, notice also how the income account never declines in value—even when the account value does. While an increase in the account value can increase the income account, a decrease in the account value has no impact on the income account.

A GLWB can allow you to take much more than you would without a GLWB.

In this example, at age seventy, you would be able to withdraw $7,865 per year. Remember, this comes from your actual account value, which in this example is $110,000 by the end at that point. That means you are allowed to take 7.15 percent of your account value.

$7,865/$110,000 = 7.15 percent

Very few, if any, financial advisors would recommend that you ever take out 7.15 percent of your retirement account—even at age seventy. Such a large withdrawal percentage creates too big of a risk that you will run out of money before you die. But when you have a GLWB on your annuity, you can do this without concern of running out of income. In fact, this is the very guarantee you are buying when you add a GLWB to your annuity. That's why I think of it as buying insurance on your future retirement income.

BUYING A LIVING BENEFIT ON A VARIABLE ANNUITY VERSUS AN INDEXED ANNUITY—IT DOES MATTER

So how likely is it that the account value will increase faster than the income base? It depends on the type of annuity. If you purchase the GLWB on an indexed annuity, it's not very likely at all. In fact, at today's expected returns on this conservative annuity design, the income account will almost always grow faster than the actual account value. However, a variable annuity is another story. With a variable annuity, you have the power of the stock market driving your returns. Achieving a return of more than 5 percent net of fees is entirely possible. However, the longer you go without a step-up, the less likely it becomes. Remember, the income account will

> GOOD PERFORMANCE EARLY IN THE CONTRACT BECOMES YOUR BEST PATH TO GETTING AN INCREASE IN FUTURE INCOME.

grow every year. If the account value falls in year one, then you must earn much more than 5 percent net of fees in year two in order to get a step-up. The bigger the gap between your actual account value and the income base, the harder it becomes to get a step-up. On the other hand, each time you get a step-up, the income base resets to equal the account value, which in turn resets your chances of getting future step-ups. Good performance early in the contract becomes your best path to getting an increase in future income.

Since you can increase your income by buying a living benefit on a variable annuity, but are highly unlikely to see the same result if you buy a living benefit on an indexed annuity, does that mean you should never add a GLWB on an indexed annuity? If only it were that simple. Think about the risk the insurance company is taking here. All your income initially comes from your own money. The insurance company only has to begin making the payments out of its pocket when your account value goes to $0. The risk to the insurance company grows as your account value falls in value relative to your income account. Withdrawals obviously reduce your account value on both an indexed and a variable annuity. However, a decline in the market can also make the account value of a variable annuity fall. A

30 percent drop in the stock market will greatly increase the chance that your account value will eventually go to $0. That is not the case with an indexed annuity. You will never earn less than 0 percent in any year on an indexed annuity. The design of the product means that your account value will not fall, even if the index your annuity return is based upon drops in value. The reality is that offering a living benefit on an indexed annuity is far less risky to the insurance company than offering a living benefit on a variable annuity. As a result, the insurance company will initially guarantee about 10–20 percent more income initially through a GLWB on an indexed annuity than a variable annuity. They will accomplish this in one or more of the following three ways:

1. They will grow the income account faster on an indexed annuity compared to a variable annuity. For example, while the income account will likely grow at 5 percent on a variable annuity, it may grow at 6–8 percent on an indexed annuity.
2. The payout will be greater on the indexed annuity. If a living benefit on a variable annuity will pay you 5 percent of the income account at age sixty-five, an indexed annuity might pay you 5.5–6 percent.
3. The income account might grow longer on an indexed annuity. Most variable annuities will only grow your income account for ten to twelve years. Some indexed annuities might grow the income account for up to twenty years.

Let's look at an example of what these differences might mean in actual income using the following assumptions:

- The buyer of both contracts is fifty-five years old and plans to start income at age sixty-five.

- $100,000 goes into both annuities; therefore, they both start with an income account equal to 100,000.
- The income base on the variable annuity grows at 5 percent.
- The income base on the indexed annuity grows at 6 percent.
- The payout on the variable annuity at age sixty-five is 5 percent.
- The payout on the indexed annuity at age sixty-five is 6 percent.

ANNUITY INCOME BASE: VARIABLE VS INDEXED

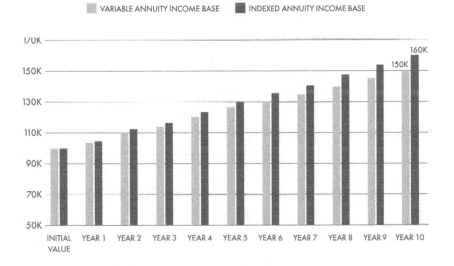

VARIABLE ANNUITY INCOME BASE   INDEXED ANNUITY INCOME BASE

- Income on the variable annuity at age sixty-five:
- 150,000 x .05 = $7,500
- Income on the indexed annuity at age sixty-five:
- 160,000 x .06 = $9,600

You can see how the indexed annuity provides more guaranteed income at the time of purchase. But does that make it the better deal? It depends. While $9,600 per year is clearly better than $7,500 per year, since the indexed annuity will likely never get a step-up, someone starting the income at age sixty-five should assume he or she will never get more than $9,600 per year. The variable annuity, on the other hand, can get a step-up. Given the lower payout of 5 percent, the income account of the variable annuity would have to rise to 192,000 in order to provide an equivalent amount of income that is guaranteed under the indexed annuity (192,000 x .05 = $9,600). How confident are you that the $100,000 investment, net of fees, will grow to at least $192,000 by the end of the tenth year? To do that, you would have to average about 7 percent per year. If you like that likelihood, then the variable annuity might make sense for you despite the lower initial guaranteed income. However, if you don't want to take that chance and you are satisfied with the $7,500 in income that you know you will get from the indexed annuity, then why bother with the uncertainty that comes with the variable annuity?

THE BEST STRATEGY ONCE YOU ADD A LIVING BENEFIT TO YOUR VARIABLE ANNUITY

If you stop to think about it, what you realize is that when you add a GLWB to an annuity contract, you are purchasing a minimum known amount of income in the future, no matter what type of annuity you purchase. Because you know the rate at which the income account will grow and you know the income payout rate is any specific age, you can calculate on day one the amount of minimum income you will have a year from now, five years from now, or ten years from now. The only question is, Will the potential growth on the variable annuity lead to more income, and if so, how much? And the only way you get more is to get a step-up. That means the goal becomes to grow the account value as much as possible as fast as possible. But does it matter if the account value goes down? Not really. While no one likes to get a statement that says they have less money than they had before, if you are purchasing the annuity with the GLWB for income in the future, the only thing that really matters is how much income you will get. Therefore, your best strategy is to invest your account value as aggressively as you can. This is completely contrary to the conventional wisdom that says you should become more conservative as you get closer to retirement. But in this case, by buying the living benefit, you have already bought insurance on the effects of a drop in your account value. Your account value could go from $100,000 to $0 prior to starting your income, and you would still get $6,875 per year for life. But if you want more income—and who doesn't?—then the only way to do that with an annuity is to grow the account value faster than the income account.

Of course, this strategy can completely backfire on you if you never turn on the income, but then I would have to question why you bought the GLWB in the first place. Why ensure your income if you are not sure you are going to even need the income?

If you are adding a GLWB on a variable annuity for the future income, it really doesn't matter if your account value goes down in value. A decline in value never leads to less income. But an increase in value might give you more income. Therefore, your best investment strategy is to invest in a way that is likely to grow your account value as much and as fast as possible.

THE INSURANCE COMPANIES UNDERSTAND THE RISK OF THIS STRATEGY

Remember, the hope of the insurance company is that you die before your account value goes to $0. In that case, they have collected your annual fees for the GLWB and never had to pay a claim. Therefore, they don't want to see your account value drop too far below your income account. Since an indexed annuity can't drop in value from year to year, the insurance company doesn't have to worry about the account value getting too far below the income account. That is not true with a variable annuity. A 30 percent or higher drop in the account value in a given year will create a large gap between the income account and the account value, thereby increasing the likelihood that the insurance company will have to begin paying your income out of its own funds.

In order to protect against this possibility, all but one or two companies will restrict how you can invest your money in the variable account if you add a living benefit. For example, they might require that you put at least 30 percent of the money in one or more bond funds and/or not allow you to put money into the most aggressive stock funds. In other words, they will attempt to smooth out your earnings and limit your downside. While this makes perfect sense for them as a means to mitigate their risk, for the reasons discussed above,

SHOULD YOU ELECT TO BUY A LIVING BENEFIT ON A VARIABLE ANNUITY, CHOOSE ONE THAT HAS THE FEWEST INVESTMENT RESTRICTIONS.

it is contrary to your goal—which is to grow your account value as much as you can, as fast as you can. You already paid for the insurance on your retirement income when you agreed to purchase the living benefit on the annuity at an extra cost. There is no reason to pay twice in the form of agreeing to restricting your investment options. Should you elect to buy a living benefit on a variable annuity, choose one that has the fewest investment restrictions. No restrictions at all are your best possible option.

FOLLOW THE RULES OF ANY LIVING BENEFIT— IT WILL COST YOU IF YOU DON'T

It probably won't surprise you to learn that there can be some pretty strict rules around any GLWB. Guaranteeing an income for life is a risky proposition for the insurance company, therefore, such a guarantee is going to come with some conditions. Here are the main rules to know and understand.

Don't Make Withdrawals until You Plan to Start the Income

Virtually all GLWBs will grow your income account until you "begin taking income." That's typically how the client brochure will describe this condition. What the brochure may or may not say is what constitutes as "taking income." In most cases, any withdrawal will be considered taking income. Therefore, while the contract will likely allow you to take up to 10 percent of your account value each year without any charges, this withdrawal is likely to stop the 5–7 percent growth that is being added to your income account each year. If the income account stops growing, the income stops growing as well. If you have an unexpected need for cash, don't tap your annuity with a GLWB until you verify whether such a withdrawal is considered income under the living benefit.

Don't Take Out More Than the GLWB Allows Each Year

If your GLWB allows you to take 5 percent of the income account each year, do not take out more than that. If you do, you will have done what the contract will call an "excess withdrawal." The consequences of an excess withdrawal range from bad to very bad to horrific depending upon your contract. I mentioned earlier in this chapter that as long as you don't take out more than what the GLWB allows, the income account does not fall, which in turn means your annual income does not fall. If you take out more than this allowable with-drawal—for example, the 5 percent—then the insurance company is going to reduce your income base. In some products, it might drop by just the amount of the excess withdrawal. In other products, it might be reduced all the way to the account value—even if that value is 30 percent lower (or more). A reduction in the income account means a reduction in your future income each year. The only question is by how much. It might be a little or it might be a lot.

Insurance Companies Retain the Right to Increase the Fees on Your GLWB

Insurance companies have to make a lot of assumptions to price out a GLWB. They have to make assumptions about the average return on your account, interest rates, your life expectancy, and when and if you plan to start taking the income. It's a given that at least one of these assumptions will be wrong. Being a little wrong is OK. They can plan for that. Being a lot wrong can put the financial well-being of the company at risk. Therefore, they have all built in the ability to periodically increase how much you have to pay each year for the GLWB. What triggers the flexibility to increase your costs varies from contract to contract. Make sure you understand how high this fee can go (there will be a limit) and under what conditions it can get there.

Having said that, this is one situation where the fees might not really matter. Remember, the income account is not money. Therefore, the fee does not come from that account. It comes from your account value. If you bought the annuity with the GLWB to get an income for life, the amount of income you get is only impacted by the fee in one way—and it really only applies to variable annuities. In order to get a step-up in your income account, the account value net of fees must be higher than the income account on your policy anniversary.

The higher your fees, the less likely you are going to get a step-up. But this probably matters only until you begin taking income. Once you start taking withdrawals, it would take a year of amazing returns for your account value to grow beyond your income account. The withdrawals do not reduce your income account (assuming it's not an excess withdrawal), but they certainly reduce your account value. After you've started your income, your account value net of fees and the annual withdrawal have to grow beyond your income account. The stock market may do really well during the first couple of years you take withdrawals—it could happen—but beyond that, it is highly unlikely.

Don't Wait Too Long to Start Taking Income

Another way to think about a GLWB is that you are paying for the right to have a guaranteed systematic withdrawal equal to 5–6 percent of your income account. The insurance company is agreeing to let you withdraw that percentage every year even if you run out of money. The longer you wait to start taking the income, the less likely it is you will take enough withdrawals to ever liquidate your account. Essentially, you are then paying for the right to take your own money. There is value to that right. After all, who knows how long you are going to live. If advances in medical science allow you to live to 110, you are likely to run out of money even if you don't start taking the income from your annuity until age eighty-five. However, until those medical advances materialize, you have to assume you are going to live a more

THE RULE OF THUMB HERE IS VERY SIMPLE: WHEN YOU NEED MORE INCOME IN RETIREMENT, TAKE IT FROM THE PRODUCT YOU PURCHASED TO PROVIDE YOU AN INSURED INCOME—THE ANNUITY WITH THE GLWB.

normal life. The fact of the matter is that if you don't start taking the income under the GLWB from your annuity prior to age seventy-five, you probably never needed to buy the GLWB in the first place.

The rule of thumb here is very simple: when you need more income in retirement, take it from the product you purchased to provide you an insured income—the annuity with the GLWB. If you know that the income from your annuity will only grow by waiting another year, it becomes tempting to take the income from other assets. However, the older you get, the higher the probability that you will die before you have fully liquidated the annuity. You're paying each year to guarantee a certain level of income from the annuity, so I always recommend that you use the annuity for the reason you purchased it—to get an income for life.

COVERING LONG-TERM CARE EXPENSES WITH LONG-TERM CARE QUALIFIED ANNUITIES

If I was asked to vote for the most underappreciated type of annuity, I would not hesitate to vote for the long-term care qualified annuity. This relatively unknown and obscure category of annuities was created by the Pension Protection Act of 2006. The goal of this part of that tax bill was to help address the growing issue state and local governments are facing to cover the cost of long-term care for individuals with no financial means. According to researchers at HealthView Services, for a sixty-five-year-old couple, there is a 75 percent chance that at least one of them will need long-term care. And despite what many people believe, Medicare does not cover long-term care. By creating a specific annuity with unique tax benefits, the hope was that people would buy long-term care qualified annuities to cover this future cost.

Most long-term care qualified annuities are essentially fixed annuities. However, there are several very important differences:

1. Unlike traditional annuities, any money withdrawn from a long-term care qualified annuity to cover long-term care

costs is not taxable. It comes out of the contract completely income-tax free. I'll bet that grabbed your attention.

2. Because interest rates are so low, most contracts pay little if any interest each year. Instead, the insurance company gives you a multiple of your initial investment in long-term care benefits. For example, you might buy a contract with $100,000 and have $200,000–$300,000 of available funds to pay for long-term care expenses. Rather than adding interest to your account each year, the insurance company essentially provides you a pool of funds to use for long-term care expenses—all completely income-tax free.

In many ways, this type of annuity is similar to life insurance. When you buy a life insurance policy, you pay either a single premium or a series of premiums in exchange for an insurance company's promise to pay an amount much larger than the premium to your beneficiary upon your death. The insurance company hopes you stay alive long enough to make enough money on your premium to cover both the cost of the death benefit and some extra amount as a profit for them. Long-term care qualified annuities work the same way. The insurance company hopes that it's many years until you need to take money out to cover long-term care costs. Better yet, you don't need long-term care at all. But if you do, you have a big pot of money available to cover such expenses.

But here is where a long-term care qualified annuity can really shine. What if you have a nonqualified annuity (one outside of a retirement account) that you've owned for years, and you don't antici-pate needing for retirement income? Eventually, either you or your beneficiaries will have to pay taxes on the income that has grown tax-deferred in the account. Remember though, you can exchange one annuity for another without creating any taxes (a 1035 tax-free exchange). A long-term care qualified annuity might have different tax treatment when used for long-term care expenses, but it's still an annuity. Therefore, it too can be purchased with the proceeds from another annuity. That means if you someday have long-term care expenses, you could tap all your already-earned, tax-deferred income completely income-tax free.

A LONG-TERM CARE QUALIFIED ANNUITY MIGHT HAVE DIFFERENT TAX TREATMENT WHEN USED FOR LONG-TERM CARE EXPENSES, BUT IT'S STILL AN ANNUITY.

Let's look at an example. Let's assume you bought a variable annuity ten years ago with a $50,000 premium. Over the years, that annuity has grown and is now worth $100,000. You have no long-term care coverage, and you don't want to have to worry about this potentially large and unknown expense in retirement. You therefore exchange your existing variable annuity for a long-term care qualified annuity. This $100,000 buys you $250,000 in long-term care coverage. This means you now have a $250,000 pot of money you can access income-tax free in the event you need it. And what if you stay healthy enough that you don't need long-term care? Congratulations! You're one of the lucky ones. All that means is that either you or your beneficiary will have to pay taxes on the $50,000 you would have paid taxes on anyway. The only thing you have given up is the potential growth on the $100,000 that you used to buy the policy. Granted, if you live long enough the growth you gave up might be substantial, but you've covered a very likely and potentially very large risk. Essentially the growth you gave up was the cost of insuring the long-term care risk.

Important Things to Know

1. With any long-term care qualified annuity, there are two parts to your account value. The first part is your premium, plus interest, if any, that is credited to your account. The second part is the extra long-term care coverage sometimes referred to as the "continuation of benefits value." When accessing your account to cover long-term care expenses, all withdrawals first come out of your deposit, plus interest. In other words, you have to use your money first. The additional coverage paid out of the insurance company's pocket begins only once you have exhausted all your own funds. Regardless of the account used, all payments are income-tax free.

2. Typically, you will have coverage for five years. Therefore, there is a limit to how much you can take out for long-term care costs each month. That limit is your total coverage divided by sixty months. In other words, if you have $240,000 in total coverage, you can take out $4,000 per month for sixty straight months.

WHAT HAPPENS IF AN ANNUITY COMPANY GOES OUT OF BUSINESS?

Relative to other types of investments, annuities are designed to be held for a much longer period of time. Certainly, if you have bought the annuity to provide yourself with an income for life, there is no longer term than your entire lifetime. So what happens if your annuity company runs into financial difficulties? How would that likely impact the promises that company made to you, if at all? Each state has its own state guarantee fund for insurance and annuities. These funds exist to compensate policyholders within the state for any losses they might incur as a result of an insurance company insolvency. Every annuity company that does business in that state must be a member of that state's guarantee association and must therefore contribute to that state's fund. Therefore, the good news is that while there is no federal insurance such as FDIC insurance provided for banks, there is a state insurance fund that operates in a similar manner.

The policyowner's state of residence—not the jurisdiction in which the contract was purchased—dictates which state guarantee association rules apply. The amount of coverage varies from state to state, but "withdrawal and cash values of annuities are covered up to at least $100,000 per person per company" according to the National Organization of Life & Health Insurance Guaranty Associations (NOLHGA). It is not uncommon, however, for some states to cover up to $500,000, and you can find a complete list of the individual coverage by state at http://www.nolhga.com/.

It's highly likely that you have never heard of this insurance even if you already own an annuity. Interestingly, state insurance regulations prohibit insurance agents and financial advisors from talking about the guarantee association at the time of sale. If you ask about the guarantee association, advisors are allowed to refer you to the NOLHGA website, but by law, their guidance must end there. The theory behind this rule is that less financially secure insurance companies might extol the virtues of the state guarantee funds in order to sell more annuities, despite their questionable financial strength. This in turn could create a potential liability for the larger, more secure insurance companies since they would have to provide funds to bail out their competitor. Personally, I find this logic hard to follow. People need lifetime income. Why create another barrier to providing this income by not allowing those advising the clients to set their minds at ease regarding the potential risk of counting on a company to make payments for you for years if not decades? In addition, banks commonly stress that they are FDIC insured. Talking about the virtues of FDIC insurance has never in itself led to a wave of bank failures. Why would the insurance industry have a different experience? Either the guarantee exists, or it does not. Obviously, it does, so why not give policyholders the peace of mind that comes with that knowledge?

How Does the State Guarantee Association Work?

Should a state insurance department decide that an insurance company has become or soon will become insolvent and incapable of paying future claims, the state insurance department will take over the company and put it into "rehabilitation." No rehabilitation process is ever the same, so I can't tell you definitively how this process would work for you should you find yourself saddled with a failed annuity company. Should you inquire with your individual state guarantee association about the process or anything else regarding the association, it will refer you to a bunch of vaguely written statutes. You will rarely, if ever, get any definitive answers to any "what if" question you might have. I believe these rules are purposely vague in order to give each state the necessary flexibility to handle each unique situation. However, we can look at previous situations as a guide for what is likely to happen. Fortunately, few examples of annuity-company bankruptcy proceedings exist. However, this also means that without much precedence there is also little guidance on a likely process. Believe it or not, one example involves Baldwin United, the piano company. Back in the early 1980s, Baldwin owned two insurance companies that sold mostly fixed annuities. Unfortunately, their portfolio, which was heavily weighted with junk bonds, could not ultimately pay the interest rates guaranteed by the policies. In 1983, the insurance companies were placed into "rehabilitation" by the states of Arkansas and Indiana. These states got to experience the joy of managing the process because they happened to be the states in which the companies were domiciled. The domiciled state always has the responsibility of coordinating the efforts of all the states in which the policyholders reside. The objective of the process is to make the policyholders whole as quickly as possible. If a sound company is willing and able to take over the troubled company, the states will arrange for that to occur. If the problem is too big and therefore no company is willing to step in, then the states take over the company with the goal of nursing the company back to financial health. That can take months or years. In the case of the Baldwin United companies, it took years.

At this point it should be mentioned that the state guarantee associations have very little in cash reserves available to fix any new problem companies. As money is needed, each state assesses the member company's fee based on the premiums written in that particular state. However, there is a maximum that each company can be assessed in any one year. Therefore, if the problem is too big, it can take several years of assessments before policyholders can be made whole. That is, in fact, what happened with the Baldwin companies. Eventually, the regulators improved the financials of the companies to the point where New York–based MetLife became willing to take over the policies.

Much can be learned by the steps that state regulators took in the Baldwin case. The first step was to suspend all policyholder liquidations with three notable exceptions. They allowed 1) regular income (annuitization) payments to continue, 2) death benefits to be paid, and 3) liquidations based on financial needs. All other policyholders found their funds frozen. After that, the regulators reduced the amount of interest credited to the policyholders. Rather than getting the 12 percent or greater rates of

WHILE ALL THE POLICIES HAD CERTAIN CONTRACTUAL GUARANTEES—INCLUDING THE MINIMUM RATE OF INTEREST THAT HAD TO BE PAID—THE STATES HAVE THE RIGHT TO CHANGE THESE GUARANTEES AS PART OF THE REHABILITATION PROCESS.

interest that were originally promised, policyholders were told that they were only going to get 5.5 percent. That might sound like a really good deal today, but interest rates were much higher back in 1983. While all the policies had certain contractual guarantees—including the minimum rate of interest that had to be paid—the states have the right to change these guarantees as part of the rehabilitation process. Finally, the states of Indiana and Arkansas hired Goldman Sachs to restructure the portfolio by selling off many of the higher-yielding junk bonds and replacing them with shorter-maturity government and corporate bonds. Over time, these actions reduced the gap between the assets and liabilities of the company. Eventually, that gap was small enough that MetLife was willing to take over the policies, at which point the money once again became available for each policyholder. Each policyholder was given the option of swapping their annuity for a new MetLife annuity or simply cashing out.

Note that while policyholders had their funds frozen for a number of years and their interest rates reduced, they did continue to earn interest during the process, and no one received less money than they had put into the annuity. In fact, everyone received more than the value they had at the time of the rehabilitation.

This process tells us three important things:

1. No policyholder is likely to lose money in the strict sense of the word, but a policyholder that earns less interest than expected and can't access his or her funds might have a different perspective.
2. Contract terms can be changed if the regulators deem it a necessary step.
3. The entire process can be tedious and complex and can take years to resolve.

What about Variable Annuities?

No company with a sizeable variable annuity block has ever gone into rehabilitation. Therefore, opinions vary on what would actually happen. Prior to the invention of living benefits, the "What if a company goes under?" question as it pertains to variable annuities was simply not a big deal. Each variable annuity company has essentially two sets of assets on its balance sheet. One set is the "general account" of the company. This account holds the assets that are used to back any guaranteed liabilities such as life insurance, fixed annuities, lifetime income guarantees, etc. The insurance company can use the assets of the "general account" toward any of its guarantees. They are not segregated based on the type of liability. Each variable annuity company also has a "separate account" that holds the assets that back just the variable annuity assets. For example, if you buy a variable annuity and allocate your money between ten different mutual fund type subaccounts, all that money must be placed in the company's separate account and the funds can only be used to give money to the variable annuity policyholders should they decide to cash in their variable annuity. Since the variable annuity assets reside in the insurance company's separate account, the rehabilitation process should have little, if any, impact on variable annuity policyholders. The purpose of the separate account is to make sure the variable annuity assets are available only to the variable annuity policyholders and are therefore unencumbered by the other obligations of the insurance company. That's precisely why it is referred to as a separate account. The state (or states) running the process should allow variable annuity policyholders to continue to operate under all the terms of the contract—including getting their money on demand. The only aspect of a basic variable annuity that should require any backing from the guarantee association is the guaranteed death benefit. In situations where the death benefit exceeds the value of the account value, the difference is paid out of the insurance company's general account, thereby creating a potential liability for the guarantee association. However, I suspect most policyholders will just want to get out of a failed insurance company. Sticking around to maintain a benefit that is not payable until the policyholder's death is not likely to be a priority in such a situation.

Living benefits have greatly muddied the waters in discussions about addressing bankruptcy. Like the guaranteed death benefits, the insurance company's living benefit guarantees are backed by the general account, not the separate account. Remember, with a living benefit such as a GLWB, should your account value go to $0 before you die, the insurance company must continue payments out of its own assets. These payments would come from the general account, not the separate account. Therefore, one would assume that any shortfall of these guarantees would be covered by the state guarantee fund. In fact, NOLHGA's website indicates that this is indeed the case. The FAQ section states, "Generally speaking, a variable annuity contract with general account guarantees will be eligible for guaranty association coverage, subject to applicable limits and exclusions on coverage." It sounds reassuring until they go on to give themselves a way out. The very next sentence of the FAQ states the following: "However, specific questions regarding coverage will be determined by the applicable guaranty association based on the terms of the contract, other relevant facts, and the guaranty association law in effect at the time of insolvency."

I translate that as follows: "Variable annuity living benefits are covered unless we decide they are not." The real problem here is that the statutes indicate that annuity "benefits" are covered, but the term "benefit" is undefined. Are death and living benefits true "benefits," as defined by the statute? And if so, how is the value of these benefits determined?

Let's begin by looking at this logically. Whether it is a fixed annuity or a variable annuity, the goal will be the same—don't allow policyholders to lose money. But what constitutes losing money on a living benefit? The policyholder most certainly hasn't lost any money prior to receiving the income under the living benefit. Up to then, it works like any other annuity, accumulating based on the returns credited to the account value. Keep in mind also that even when you start taking income under the living benefit, you are initially receiving your own money.

You will not incur a "loss" until the lifetime income withdrawals deplete the account values and the insurance company is required to continue payments from its general account. Even if the income account of the living benefit is significantly higher than the account value and would therefore provide an amount of income that will liquidate your actual account value well before your life expectancy, the account value is not likely to be liquidated until ten or more years after the income begins. It seems unlikely to me that the guarantee associations are going to find it necessary to provide money to a policyholder who may or may not have a loss years down the road.

The same is true regarding any death benefits. No actual benefit is due until the designated person, usually the annuitant, dies. It seems equally unlikely to me that the guarantee association is going to provide money to cover a benefit that may or may not occur in the future. If they do choose to make good on these guarantees, they will likely require the policyholder to keep the policy in force and then pay out any shortfall from these benefits if and when it becomes necessary.

To get an idea of how this might work, we could look at a company that is currently working through the rehabilitation process.

Penn Treaty Network America Insurance Company (Penn Treaty) is a long-term care company (mostly) that was placed into rehabilitation by the state insurance department of Pennsylvania back in 2009. More than ten years later, despite the fact that two of the company's subsidiaries were placed into liquidation in 2017, the states handling the rehabilitation has still not assessed any member insurance companies to cover losses. The state has simply used Penn Treaty's existing assets to pay claims as they came due. However, eventually, it seems likely that Penn Treaty will run out of assets before it satisfies all its liabilities. While this is a long-term care company and not a variable annuity company, the process the state followed may be instructive. Like a long-term care company, an annuity company with living benefits on the books will experience the actual losses due to the benefits over time. Even in the worst financial situation, it will be a long time until the company runs out of assets to cover the liabilities. Therefore, it will be tempting for the state insurance department to just kick the can down the road for as long as possible.

The real question could very well be, Will the policyholder be allowed to begin to receive or continue to receive income payments from the living benefit at all? Such income payments are really just systematic withdrawals that are guaranteed for life (assuming the withdrawal rules are followed). As mentioned previously, the first thing the regulators typically do is suspend withdrawals. They would have to elect to make an exception for withdrawals received as a result of the living benefit. This could be even more problematic for variable annuity assets. Since variable annuity assets are part of the company's separate account, they could certainly justify this distinction. However, there could be significant political pressure on them not to make an exception. Fixed annuity policyholders are typically older, more conservative, and less wealthy than variable annuity policyholders. How would it play in the press if the insurance department prohibited the eighty-year-old grandmother from making a withdrawal from her fixed annuity but allowed the sixty-two-year-old upper-middle-class variable annuity policyholder to withdraw funds without restrictions?

HOW WOULD IT PLAY IN THE PRESS IF THE INSURANCE DEPARTMENT PROHIBITED THE EIGHTY-YEAR-OLD GRANDMOTHER FROM MAKING A WITHDRAWAL FROM HER FIXED ANNUITY BUT ALLOWED THE SIXTY-TWO-YEAR-OLD UPPER-MIDDLE-CLASS VARIABLE ANNUITY POLICYHOLDER TO WITHDRAW FUNDS WITHOUT RESTRICTIONS?

My argument is that the proper solution would be to restrict policyholders with living benefits to just the income that is available through the living benefit. That strikes me as the logical conclusion. However, I would refer you back to the statement that "specific questions regarding coverage will be determined by the applicable guaranty association."

It Is impossible to predict how annuities with or without living benefits will be treated until the industry witnesses a situation where some of the theories presented in this chapter are put to the test in an actual case. With luck, that will never occur. The fact of the matter is that such situations are very rare. And to date, the industry can continue to claim that one way or another, the industry has always met all its obligations.

QUESTIONS TO ASK AND THINGS TO LOOK OUT FOR

We live in a world full of choices. Whether it be Oreos, toothpaste, or annuities—they all come in various sizes, types, and flavors. Unfortunately, this also means there are likely to be some bad choices as well. While I can satisfy my need for an Oreo cookie with many of the multitude of flavors that exist today, a cheap knockoff store-brand cookie might leave me with nothing but empty calories. It's no different with annuities. You don't need to find the "best" annuity to meet a financial goal. Any number of the choices available today can help protect your retirement assets and/or your retirement income. However, a poorly designed annuity or an annuity bought for the wrong reasons can prove very costly. If you look out for the following things, you will greatly reduce the chances that you will later suffer buyer's remorse.

Be Wary of Any Financial Advisor Who Thinks Everyone Should Own an Annuity

There are financial advisors and insurance agents who focus heavily on annuities. That in itself is not a bad thing. After all, if I'm going to have heart surgery, I'm going to go to a heart surgeon, not a general practitioner. But there's a difference between being an annuity expert and an annuity salesperson. The expert will lay out the pros and the cons and will also compare and contrast the annuity solution to alternative product solutions. The annuity salesman will focus only on the benefits of an annuity. He or she will make the annuity sound like the answer to all your prayers.

THERE'S A DIFFERENCE BETWEEN BEING AN ANNUITY EXPERT AND AN ANNUITY SALESPERSON.

Bottom line is that if you feel as though you are being sold, get a second opinion.

Ask What the Commission Is on the Annuity

As I mentioned in a previous chapter, insurance companies learned long ago that the higher the commission, the more motivated an individual is to recommend the annuity. While annuity commissions have generally come down over the last ten to fifteen years, there are still annuities that have been designed to maximize the compensation to the person selling the annuity. Although the insurance company doesn't deduct the commission directly from the amount you invest, you do pay that commission one way or another. This payment will come in one or a combination of three forms:

- Lower interest paid to you
- Higher fees paid by you
- A longer time period to get out of the funds without paying an early withdrawal fee (surrender charge)

As a guide, I'm going to show here the typical annuity commission ranges that I previously listed in the chapter on why people hate annuities:

- Fixed annuities: 1.5–4 percent
- Immediate annuities: 4 percent
- Indexed annuities: 3.5–5 percent
- Structured annuities: 5–6 percent
- Variable annuities: 5–7 percent

If the person recommending the annuity is quoting a commission higher than these ranges, or worse yet, won't tell you at all, ask to see an annuity with a lower commission, and then do your own comparison in terms of rates and fees.

As previously mentioned, a growing number of annuities are being sold without a commission. These annuities are being placed in an advisory account where you pay the advisor an annual fee for his or her advice. While these annuities are going to be much cheaper and/or pay better returns than the commissionable one, that does not automatically mean they are a better deal for you. Make sure you consider how the annual advisory fee impacts your net returns.

Be Wary of Any Advisor Who Believes No One Should Own an Annuity

Fisher Investments, one of the country's largest registered investment advisory firms, has built an entire campaign around the evils of annuities. If you've done a Google search on annuities, you've probably seen one of the following ads for them:

- "I Hate Annuities and You Should Too"
- "5 Reasons to Be Wary of Annuities"

Their basic premise is that the "high" costs of annuities make them an inefficient investment vehicle. If you instead give your money to Fisher Investments, their expertise in designing customized portfolios will allow you to meet your retirement goals and leave you with more money for your heirs. In most cases, they will likely be right. The key words here are "most cases." While investment advisory firms like Fisher Investments can design portfolios to provide retirement income, they can't tell you with certainty that you won't run out of money. You will hear phrases like, "If this happens ..." or "If this doesn't happen ..." or "If you don't live much past a specific age ... then you will be fine."

WHILE INVESTMENT ADVISORY FIRMS LIKE FISHER INVESTMENTS CAN DESIGN PORTFOLIOS TO PROVIDE RETIREMENT INCOME, THEY CAN'T TELL YOU WITH CERTAINTY THAT YOU WON'T RUN OUT OF MONEY.

Firms like Fisher Investments that shun annuities completely will also tell you that they are a fiduciary and therefore are required to put your interests ahead of their own. In other words, they are not allowed to recommend a commissionable product because that would create a conflict of interest for them. If I'm getting paid a commission to sell you something, am I recommending it because it's what you need or because of the commission I will receive? And even if an annuity is the right choice for you, am I recommending one annuity over another because one of them pays more commission than the other? But don't let the fancy term "fiduciary" lull you into a false sense of security. While it's true that firms like Fisher Investments do not receive commissions and therefore qualify under the definition of a fiduciary, they are still offering conflicted advice. Quite frankly, anyone that is trying to convince you to let them manage your money is going to be conflicted in some way. In Fisher Investments' case, they want to convince you not to buy an annuity and give your money to them to manage. Or, if you have an annuity, they want to convince you to cash in the annuity and give the proceeds to them. They will be able to charge their annual advisory fee only if you give them your money. The bottom line is that no financial advisor works for free. Whether it be a commission or an ongoing advisory fee, the financial advisor and insurance agent will only get paid if you follow his or her recommendation.

Beware of Bonus Annuities

Some annuities offer to pay you a bonus when you buy the annuity. This bonus amount, typically 5–10 percent, is added to the value of your annuity when the policy is issued. This design is typically found in fixed and fixed indexed annuities, although there are still some bonus variable annuities as well. On the surface, this seems like a really good deal. Who wouldn't want to get paid extra just to buy the annuity? It's almost like getting a commission on your own annuity contract. Spoiler alert: Insurance companies are not in the habit of just giving away money. If they pay you a bonus, they are going to want something in return. You can expect the bonus to come with one or more of the following requirements:

- You are likely to have a much longer surrender charge period. Paying you a bonus is indeed like paying more commission. Therefore, it's going to take the insurance company more years to recover the policy issue costs. This in turn leads to a longer surrender charge period—likely ten to fifteen years.
- The bonus will vest over time—probably ten years. Rather than extend the surrender charge period, they might claw back

the bonus should you get out before the vesting period ends. This is really just a different way to recover the bonus should you get out of the annuity too soon.

- If there are fees assessed on the annuity each year, the bonus will add to those fees. This method is most likely to be seen in a variable annuity.

Let me now say that a bonus annuity is not necessarily bad. In fact, if you stay in the annuity a long time, you will often end up with more money in a bonus annuity than a non-bonus annuity. The reason for this is quite simple. The insurance companies know that a certain percentage of the purchasers will indeed get out of the annuity before the end of the surrender charge period and/or the vesting period. The insurance company does not end up paying the full bonus to these policyholders. The carriers therefore factor early liquidations into the amount of the bonus they pay. This means policyholders that stay in benefit from those that don't.

One last thing on this topic. If someone is recommending that you liquidate your existing annuity that still has a surrender charge and that you should then buy a bonus annuity in order to recover all or some of those surrender charges, simply say no and walk away. Why incur any of the above bulleted requirements just to get out of an existing annuity early?

A FEW RANDOM, BUT IMPORTANT, ISSUES

Over the years, I've unfortunately seen far too many problems that were mostly a result of ignorance regarding a few quirky things about how annuities work. Fortunately, these situations are relatively rare, but when they do occur, the outcome can be very harmful to the policyholder. The tips in this chapter will help you avoid being one of the unfortunate few.

Keep the Annuity Structure Simple

In addition to the insurance company, every annuity has three parties to the contract:

- The owner is the person or persons (in the event of a joint owner) that actually own and control the annuity. The value and all the benefits of the contract belong to the owner(s) as long as they are alive. The owner(s) controls the policy and is the sole party that can make changes, take money out or terminate the contract.

- The annuitant is the individual whom the annuity is based on. Because every annuity has the option of paying an income for life, that income must be based on a living individual. This party is referred to as the annuitant because any lifetime annuity payments are based on this person. In most cases, the owner and the annuitant are the same. In fact, I strongly recommend that, unless it's simply not possible, the owner and annuitant always be the same person. If you follow this advice, you will greatly reduce the chances that you, or your beneficiary, will experience unintended consequences. More on that in a minute.

- The beneficiary is the person or persons who will get the proceeds of the annuity upon the death of either the owner or annuitant, depending upon how the contract defines the life that triggers the death benefit. Annuities also give the option of naming a contingent beneficiary that will receive the proceeds in the event the primary beneficiary is no longer alive.

I always recommend one of the following two structures. The first structure is for a single owner and the second is if you want a joint owner—for example, you and your spouse.

SINGLE-OWNER STRUCTURE:

- Owner: You
- Annuitant: You
- Beneficiary: Your spouse (or kids/charity, etc.)
- Contingent beneficiary: Whoever you want to get the money if you and the beneficiary were to unexpectedly die together

JOINT-OWNER STRUCTURE:

- Owners: You and your spouse
- Joint annuitants: You and your spouse
- Beneficiaries: You and your spouse
- Contingent beneficiary: Whoever you want to get the money if both you and your spouse die together

Originally, every annuity would pay the beneficiary upon the death of the annuitant rather than the owner. In most cases, the owner and annuitant were one and the same, so it didn't matter who died first. However, financial planners began to recommend that the annuitant be someone really young, like a grandchild. That allowed the taxes to be deferred for as long as the grandchild was alive. People began to use annuities to avoid taxes through multiple generations. Not surprisingly, the IRS was not a fan of this approach. They want to get their taxes sooner rather than later. Therefore, in the 1980s, they changed the tax code to say that the death benefit must be paid upon the "death of the holder" of the contract. Unfortunately, this tax law change did not define who the "holder" was. Most insurance companies defined the "holder" as the owner. But others chose for various reasons to define the "holder" as the annuitant. As long as the owner and the annuitant were the same, it didn't matter. But, if they were different, unintended consequences could occur. Take the following structure as an example:

- Owner: You (or you and your spouse)
- Annuitant: Your grandson
- Beneficiary: Your daughter

Your likely intent with this structure was to create a contract that could exist as long as your grandson is alive and have the contract go to your daughter as the beneficiary upon your death. If the contract defined you, as the owner, to be the "holder" of the contract, this would work. When you—the holder/owner—die, the ownership of the contract will pass to your spouse as the co-owner. If there is no co-owner, then the proceeds would be paid to your daughter as the beneficiary. But if the contract defined the "holder" as the annuitant, and the grandson died prior to you, the money would have to be paid to your daughter even though you were still alive. Worse yet, because you were still alive, the tax code would actually say that you have made a taxable gift to your daughter when she receives the death benefit. As if all of this wasn't bad enough, if you did not name a contingent owner, and you died first, the contract might specify that the annuitant—your grandson—is the beneficiary of the owner if the owner dies prior to the annuitant. If this were the case, then the proceeds of the contract would go to your grandson rather than your daughter. Confused? You would be far from alone. I will advise again: keep things simple and just avoid this situation.

To be sure, there are some valid reasons to have the owner and annuitant be different persons. The most common reason is when the owner is too old to be the annuitant. Most insurance companies will only issue annuities to someone below the age of eighty-five. But, if at all possible, stick to one of the structures I've listed above. If you truly believe (or your advisor does) that you need a different structure

TO BE SURE, THERE ARE SOME VALID REASONS TO HAVE THE OWNER AND ANNUITANT BE DIFFERENT PERSONS.

than what I've suggested, make sure you understand what happens upon the death of any party to the contract. And get it in writing from the insurance company issuing the contract. It's not unheard of that an insurance company's customer service rep is not completely familiar with how the death claims would work on every contract that is issued by the company and would therefore give you an incorrect answer.

Should I Put an Annuity in a Trust?

Increasingly, I see annuities purchased within someone's trust. On the surface, this seems completely logical. For a variety of valid reasons, many individuals hold the bulk of their assets in a trust, since that's where the assets are held and an annuity is often one of the trust assets. But that in itself is not a reason to buy an annuity in a trust. Three common reasons for establishing a trust are to avoid probate, protect your assets from creditors,

AS LONG AS YOU DON'T NAME A BENEFICIARY AN INDIVIDUAL OR ENTITY OTHER THAN YOUR ESTATE, THE ANNUITY WILL ALWAYS AVOID PROBATE.

and control the assets after you die. However, an annuity can often accomplish all three of these goals without the creation of a trust. As long as you don't name a beneficiary an individual or entity other than your estate, the annuity will always avoid probate. In addition, most annuity companies will let you put payout restrictions on your beneficiary designation, thereby making it impossible for the beneficiary to receive the money as a lump sum upon your death. And finally, in many states, annuities provide creditor protection. You should check with an attorney about the rules in your state.

Trusts are also often used as a means to reduce the size of an individual's estate at death, thereby reducing potential estate taxes. However, this is only accomplished if you set up an irrevocable trust, which means you effectively give up control of the assets. Once you place an asset in an irrevocable trust, it is no longer your asset. This rule would apply to every asset in the trust—even the annuity. Therefore, if the goal is to reduce your estate, you gain nothing toward this goal by buying an annuity within the irrevocable trust and naming the trust as the owner of the annuity.

There are some valid reasons for buying an annuity within a trust. The single best reason is that an annuity can greatly reduce the taxes a trust must pay each year. It takes very little income to be generated by a trust in order to be taxed at the highest tax bracket. For example, in 2022, any income over $13,450 would be taxed at 37 percent. By contrast, single-filing taxpayers don't hit a 37 percent tax rate until they reach $539,900 in income. However, the tax deferral of an annuity extends to annuities held within a trust. As long as the earnings remain in the annuity and are not paid out to the trust, the deferred income within the annuity itself is not taxable as income to the trust. Therefore, putting a tax-deferred annuity in the trust can help reduce the taxable income of the trust as long as the earnings remain in the annuity.

However, there are several potential problems with putting an annuity in a trust. First and foremost, the trust must be set up correctly in order to get the benefits of tax deferral. The tax code provides the benefit of tax deferral only for natural persons. For example, if a corporation buys an annuity and names itself the owner of the contract, any earnings from that annuity will be taxable each year. Since a corporation is not a "natural person," it is not entitled to the benefit of tax deferral. Obviously, a trust is not a person either, but the IRS has said that if the trust is "an agent for a natural person," then it can own an annuity and gain tax deferral. Generally, that means the trust must be a revocable living trust established for the benefit of a single individual. In addition, the beneficiary of the trust should be a surviving spouse and/or children. The tax code is unclear as to whether the annuity would be tax deferred if the beneficiary is a business or even a charity.

Second, when an annuity is purchased within a trust, it's common to see the trust listed as the beneficiary of the annuity rather than a specific individual—even if a specific individual is listed as the beneficiary of the trust. At first glance, this would seem to make sense. After all, as stated above, one purpose of a trust is to have specific payout instructions upon death. However, I've seen this create unexpected tax situations. If a spouse is the beneficiary of an annuity—even one held in a trust—that spouse has the option of taking over the annuity as the new owner and holding it as long as he or she wants. This allows the spouse to continue the tax deferral and have tremendous flexibility as to when to take the money and pay the deferred taxes. If the beneficiary is any person other than the spouse, then they can stretch the proceeds out over ten years. However, if the trust is the beneficiary, because the trust is not a person, it must liquidate the annuity over no more than five years. Further adding to the potential negative consequences is the fact that the income from the annuity will be taxable income to the trust and is therefore taxed at the income tax rate of the trust. Once again, because the trust is taxed at the highest tax bracket at such a low threshold, the end result of this structure is a high likelihood that the proceeds of the annuity will be taxed at a far higher rate than the tax rate of the beneficiary who is ultimately receiving the proceeds of the trust. The only way to avoid this is for the trust to pay out all the income at once to the trust beneficiary. Unfortunately, since most trusts put some restrictions on how the income must be paid out and over what time period, that is often prohibited by the terms of the trust itself.

And finally, if you decide to hold an annuity in a trust, it's recommended that you have the trust buy the annuity. It is possible to transfer an existing annuity into a trust, but if the transfer is not done correctly, you could end up owing taxes on all the annuity's deferred income in the year it is transferred into the trust. Essentially, you could be inadvertently liquidating the existing annuity and using the proceeds to buy another annuity.

If you already have a trust established, there are strong tax reasons to put an annuity within that trust. But if you don't, make sure you are very clear as to why you want to establish the trust in the first place. The fact of the matter is, just buying an annuity can give you the benefits that come with a trust. The annuity is already tax deferred; it already allows you to name a beneficiary; most annuity companies allow you to restrict how the beneficiary can receive the money upon your death; and it already avoids probate. On top of all that, it's much cheaper and easier to buy an annuity than to establish a trust.

If you ever are advised to put an annuity in a trust, get a second opinion. If the advice comes from your attorney, go talk to your financial advisor. If the advice comes from your financial advisor, go talk to your attorney. It's my experience that it's rare for financial advisors to know enough about trusts to make such a recommendation, and it's even rarer for attorneys to know enough about annuities to make such a recommendation. Make sure they are both on the same page as to why you need a trust and what purpose the annuity will serve within that trust.

What to Do with an Annuity in a Divorce

The go-to solution in most divorces is to just split the assets in half. There's nothing easier or a fairer outcome than each ex getting fifty shares of Apple stock or half of each mutual fund position. Unfortunately, most divorce attorneys take this same simplistic approach with annuities. On the surface it certainly makes sense. If the annuity is worth $100,000, why not divide it in half and give $50,000 to each party? There are multiple potential problems with this approach.

POSSIBLE TAX CONSEQUENCES, SURRENDER CHARGES, AND LOSS OF BENEFITS

Most insurance companies can't take a $100,000 annuity issued on March 10, 2010, as an example, and after the issue date, turn it into two $50,000 annuities as if they were both issued on March 10, 2010. Their administrative systems simply do not allow them to retroactively issue a contract. Therefore, if they get a divorce decree instructing them to "split" an annuity, they will essentially withdraw $50,000 from the contract and issue a new contract for $50,000. If the annuity is outside of a retirement account, then this "withdrawal" to fund the new annuity could be taxable to the extent of interest earned on the contract. For example, if the annuity in our hypothetical example was funded with a $60,000 payment, then $40,000 of the $50,000 deposited into the new annuity could be taxable to the owner of the contract. If the original annuity was not jointly owned, then it must be decided which spouse will be responsible for the taxes. Sadly, it's sometimes not learned that dividing the annuity creates a taxable event until after the divorce agreement is signed and the assets are divided. In such cases, the

> SADLY, IT'S SOMETIMES NOT LEARNED THAT DIVIDING THE ANNUITY CREATES A TAXABLE EVENT UNTIL AFTER THE DIVORCE AGREEMENT IS SIGNED AND THE ASSETS ARE DIVIDED.

original owner is going to be stuck with the tax bill. If, on the other hand, the annuity is held in a retirement plan such as an IRA, then

197

the taxes can be avoided by instructing the insurance company to transfer half the proceeds to the IRA of the other spouse.

But the potential problems don't stop there. If the annuity is still in the surrender charge period, then the 50 percent withdrawal will certainly exceed the allowable 10 percent annual withdrawal and could therefore be subjected to surrender charges, thereby reducing the value of the withdrawal. In addition, if it's a variable annuity, it may have a death benefit that is greatly reduced by the withdrawal.

And that's not all. The original contract most likely has benefits no longer available today. It might have a minimum interest rate of 3 percent or a living benefit that guarantees far more income than what is available today. These valuable features will remain only on the original contract. The party that gets the new contract may have the same cash value, but the loss of these key benefits can make it worth much less than the original contract that continues to be owned by the other ex-spouse.

WHAT IF THERE IS MORE THAN ONE ANNUITY?

It is not uncommon for households to own more than one annuity. I was once asked to consult on a case where the husband had purchased thirteen different annuities over the years. The combined value of these contracts was over $1.5 million. Since so much money was at stake, the wife's attorney thought it best to get some advice before just agreeing to divide each of the contracts. She also wondered if certain annuities were more valuable than others. She was wise to be cautious. Her decision to seek out advice saved her client a lot of money. Some of the annuities were in an IRA, which meant any withdrawals would be 100 percent taxable. Others were outside of a retirement plan and therefore had far less tax consequences in the event of a withdrawal. Some had very valuable living and death benefits. Others did not. I ranked each of the annuities based not only on their after-tax value, but also on the optional benefits. This gave the wife and her attorney a list to work from when negotiating as to who gets which annuity.

THE SOLUTION

My biggest piece of advice on this topic is don't assume that your divorce attorney understands anything about annuities. That is not their area of expertise. They will most likely assume an annuity is an annuity and therefore treat them like any other asset. Get the advice of a financial advisor that commonly works with annuities. Have him or her look at each contract and assess its true value before you agree to any kind of asset split.

Next, once both parties have agreed on how the annuities are to be treated, if you intend to actually split any contract in any way, first ask the insurance company how they will treat this. If you wait until after the divorce agreement is signed, the insurance company's hands will be tied by the terms of the divorce decree. If it tells them to split it fifty-fifty, that's what they will do using their own administrative procedures—taxes and benefits be damned. However, if the divorce decree instructs them to split the contracts without creating a taxable event (as an example), then they will have to find a way to do that. They can't just ignore a divorce decree simply because it is administratively difficult for them.

One possible solution is to not divide the contract at all. If the annuity is worth $100,000, then have one spouse keep the annuity (preferably the current owner) and have the other spouse get an asset of equal value. Of course, this gets us back to need to have someone value the contract. Always remember, two annuities with the same amount of money can have two very different values.

IF YOU WON THE LOTTERY, WOULD YOU TAKE THE LUMP SUM OR THE ANNUITY?

As I sit down to write this last chapter, I keep thinking about a newspaper article I just read about the most recent Powerball prize ("So You Win the $1.2B Powerball. Should You Take the Cash or Payment Plan?"). Rather than focus on the potential $1.2 billion prize, this article asked the question as to whether someone should take the $596.7 million lump sum or take the full $1.2 billion in annual payments over thirty years. In other words, a thirty-year-term certain annuity. For the record, almost everyone who wins a large lottery prize elects to take the lump sum. But should they? After

I SHOULD PROBABLY ACKNOWLEDGE THAT IT'S HARD TO MAKE A BAD CHOICE WHEN CHOOSING BETWEEN $596.7 MILLION IN CASH OR $1.2 BILLION OVER THIRTY YEARS.

all, there is a big difference between $596.7 million and $1.2 billion. The journalist who wrote the article asked a number of people what they would do. Not surprisingly, all but one individual said they would take the lump sum. It was the reasons they gave that I found intriguing. All those reasons touched on some of the negative perceptions about annuities that I covered in this book. Therefore, this seemed to be a good way to wrap up this discussion on annuities. At this point I should probably acknowledge that it's hard to make a bad choice when choosing between $596.7 million in cash or $1.2 billion over thirty years. Unless the lottery winner is incredibly bad with money (which is always possible), either choice should provide more money than anyone can spend in a lifetime. However, this book wasn't written for the mega-rich. This book was written for the person who is concerned with maintaining their current lifestyle—or better—throughout their entire lifetime. In other words, the person who has saved enough for retirement but is justifiably concerned that a health event, a significant drop in stocks, and/or just living for a long time can create challenges for their retirement plan.

Reasons Cited for Not Taking the Annuity

I CAN DO BETTER THAN THE RETURN PROVIDED BY THE ANNUITY

In order to generate the equivalent of $1.2 billion paid out annually over thirty years, the person that takes the $596.7 million lump sum would have to earn the equivalent of 4.3 percent per year for each of the thirty years. Given that historically, the long-term return of a portfolio that is 60 percent stocks and 40 percent bonds is about 8 percent, 4.3 percent doesn't seem that hard (as seen in Vanguard's article, "Like the Phoenix, the 60/40 Portfolio Will Rise Again"). Just think how much more money we would have if we earned even just 6 percent. But what if shortly after receiving and investing the

$596.7 million, the market goes down 25 percent or more? In other words, what happens if we invested the money on December 1, 2021, just before we experienced the largest drop of a balanced sixty-forty portfolio in history. How much more do we have to earn to generate the same $1.2 billion if the $596.7 million is now worth only $475 million? The answer would be about 7.5 percent. Doesn't seem so easy now, does it?

I'D RATHER TAKE THE CASH BECAUSE I DON'T THINK I'LL LIVE THE ENTIRE THIRTY YEARS

A couple of notes on this one. First, since the lottery is a thirty-year-term certain payment, the payments won't stop once the winner dies. The payments will simply continue to be paid to the listed beneficiary. However, in this case, the fifty-eight-year-old woman said she would give much of the money away and therefore wanted to control all the gifts during her lifetime. I will also note that the life expectancy of a fifty-eight-year-old woman is 26.28 years, which

> SINCE THE LOTTERY IS A THIRTY-YEAR-TERM CERTAIN PAYMENT, THE PAYMENTS WON'T STOP ONCE THE WINNER DIES.

means she has better than 50 percent chance that she won't live the full thirty years. But that also means there is at least a 40 percent chance that she will live well past the age of eighty-eight. A concern that they will die too soon and the insurance company will "win" is a major reason people elect not to pay for a lifetime income. And in fact, I've stressed previously in this book that anyone that has a short life expectancy due to health reasons is likely not a good candidate for buying a lifetime income. On the other hand, I'm sure we all know someone that has ended up living longer than expected. I had a boss once that was thrilled to turn forty-five because no male in his family had ever lived to that age. Two weeks ago we celebrated his eightieth birthday. And based on what I observed, he's got a lot of years to go. The bottom line is that because we don't know how long we're going to live, establishing a lifetime income other than social security is a great sleeping pill in retirement.

I WANT TO SPEND IT WHILE I CAN BECAUSE NOTHING IS GUARANTEED IN LIFE

This viewpoint reminds me of the J.G. Wentworth ads on TV that carry the theme: "It's my money and I want it now." J.G. Wentworth is one of the many firms that offer to buy out annuity payments from recipients that either need or just plain want the money. There is nothing guaranteed in life, so I get it. But if you take the lump sum or elect to self-fund your retirement from your own assets, you now have no guarantee that you won't start running out of money and therefore have to significantly cut back on your lifestyle. And while bad things can happen to the insurance company that is guaranteeing your lifetime income, no policyholder has missed out on a check yet. And consider one more thing. Firms like J.G. Wentworth exist to make money. They wouldn't offer to pay cash for existing annuities if they didn't believe they would get a greater return from the annuity payments than what they can earn on the cash they used to by the annuity.

The One Person That Would Take the $1.2 Billion over Thirty Years

There was one person that indicated they would not take the lump sum. Interestingly, that one person was a certified financial planner. Of all the people interviewed, he was the only one trained on how to invest. Despite this, he said he would take an annuity because it would so dramatically reduce his risk of making poor investment decisions. "It allows you to make a mistake here and there," he said. "People don't understand there is potential for loss. They only focus on the potential for gain."

And that, in a nutshell, is the primary point of the book. If you are like me and you want that sleeping pill during retirement, establishing an income for life should be part of your retirement plan. At the very least, make sure you understand the additional risks you are taking if you elect not to outsource a personal pension to an insurance company.

IF YOU ARE LIKE ME AND YOU WANT THAT SLEEPING PILL DURING RETIREMENT, ESTABLISHING AN INCOME FOR LIFE SHOULD BE PART OF YOUR RETIREMENT PLAN.

Thank You for Reading

Whether you've read this entire book or just isolated chapters, I want to thank you for reading. You likely picked up this book to get some answers on how to prepare for or navigate your finances in retirement. I hope this book gave you some clarity. More importantly, I hope it helped you sleep better and approach retirement with more confidence.

ACKNOWLEDGEMENTS

By the time this book is published, I will have finished my fortieth year in the annuity industry. There are dozens of different areas within the financial services industry. People commonly move from one to another. I never did. To stay in one relatively small slice of such a large industry is very unusual, and it certainly wasn't my original plan. I, like almost everyone who enters this industry, assumed my first job would be a stepping stone that would eventually lead to something very different. In a way, it did, just not the way I expected. I was very fortunate that two people in particular gave me the opportunity to reinvent myself without having to leave the industry.

The first of these two is Bob Saltzman, a man that I'm proud to call my mentor. In 1985, at the young and naive age of twenty-five, I interviewed at a company called Sun Life Insurance Company of America in Atlanta. Sun Life later rebranded itself as SunAmerica and is now part of the international insurance conglomerate AIG. At the time, I was working as the product manager of annuities at Edward Jones in St. Louis. Sun Life was one of the handful of annuity companies that Edward Jones represented, so I knew all the main people at Sun Life. I figured the interview would be little more than a formality. When I arrived on my interview day, I was given an agenda. As expected, I knew everyone I was meeting with—except one. That would be Bob. I didn't think much about it initially. Since I had never seen him in one of my numerous meetings with people at Sun Life, I assumed my meeting with him would be no big deal. That assumption quickly changed when I was taken to his office. It was the corner office. It was big. And it had a couch. He introduced himself as the new president of Sun Life. Even at that young age, I knew this interview had to go well. I guess it did, because I got the job. Five years later when Sun Life changed its name to SunAmerica and moved to Los Angeles, Bob offered me the job of national sales manager—quite the step-up for someone who was not yet thirty. Was I qualified? Probably not. But Bob had faith in me, so I assumed I was up to the challenge. Two years later, to say that SunAmerica had run into some customer service challenges would be an understatement. Rapid growth, combined with an inexperienced workforce and a new and heavily flawed computer system, will bring any company to its knees. Bob chose to do something really crazy. He asked me, a person with zero operations experience, to run SunAmerica's annuity operations and fix the problems. Once again, Bob had faith in me, so I assumed I was up to the task. And I was. Two years after that, Bob left SunAmerica to become the CEO of Jackson National Life. In 1995, Bob asked me to join him at Jackson in the capacity of senior VP of Life Insurance and Annuity Operations. Of course, I took him up on it. How could I not? Bob continually challenged me to do new things. For that, I'm eternally grateful.

By 2005, I had been working in the insurance company side of the annuity business for twenty years and was ready for something new and different. Enter Dennis Zank of Raymond James Financial, an investment firm in St. Petersburg, Florida (and the company that sponsors the football stadium for the Tampa Bay Bucs). Dennis hired me to be the president of Raymond James Insurance Group (RJIG). RJIG is really a wholly owned subsidiary of Raymond James and therefore is really a business within a business. For the first time, I got to do sales, marketing, product development, and operations—all in one job. My thanks to Dennis for not only giving me the best job I ever had but also for always being so willing to share his incredible wisdom, experience, and common sense. I would also be remiss not to thank Chet Helck for his help while I was at Raymond James. I knew Chet from my early days at Edward Jones. Chet was an executive VP at Raymond James when I was hired to work there. It was Chet that not only connected me with Dennis but also was one of my biggest supporters after I was hired. I owe him a lot.

You see, the opportunities that Bob, Dennis and Chet gave me kept me challenged and allowed me to continue to learn and try new things. I simply never had to leave the annuity industry to try something new.

When you're in a single industry for forty years, you can't help but have a long list of people that helped you along the way. For me it was people like Doug Kinder, Bill Barrett, Bob Cassato, Doug Wood, Scott Logan, Joe Jordan, Bernie Gacona, Beth Maziad, Mariann Carson, Vanessa Marcos, Johnna Chewning, Jim Swink, and Blair O'Connor, to name a few. My thanks to each of you. You made my various jobs fun, interesting, and rewarding. And my apologies to the countless other people that were a joy to work with over the years. There are far too many of you to mention.

But I want specifically to thank my oldest and most trusted colleague in the industry, Kevin Connor. I met Kevin just weeks after taking the annuity product manager job at Edward Jones. He worked for a wholesaling and marketing firm named PLANCO at the time. I was sent to PLANCO's home office in King of Prussia, Pennsylvania, to "learn about annuities." Kevin's been one of my best friends and confidants ever since. I'm pretty sure that Kevin and I are the only two people that are still active in the annuity industry after at least forty years.

I have to also mention my very first boss in the industry, John Beurlein. John was the general partner of Edward Jones's syndicate department when he hired me as an intern while I was still in graduate school at Washington University. While I was just a lowly intern and John was a general partner, he never made me feel like I worked for him. I always felt like I worked with him. While I only worked directly "with" him for fewer than two years, his management style influenced my management style throughout my entire career. When in doubt, I always asked myself, "How would John handle this?" Thank you, John, for everything.

Since I want to stay out of the dog house, I have to also thank my wife, Tina Corner-Stolz. Seriously though, this thank-you is the easiest of them all. Tina is my biggest cheerleader and inspires me every day. If you want to learn everything about running peer groups, check out her current book *Sit Down! Stand Up! Cash In!—A CEO's Guide to Peer Advisory Groups* and her soon-to-be-released book, *Your Seat at the Table*.

And finally, I want to thank anyone that has reached this point in the book. I hope you found it helpful in some way. If even one of you is sleeping better in retirement because of something you read in this book, it was worth the time it took to write it.